KU-766-823

# THE ART OF
# TYMPANIST AND DRUMMER

**ANDREW A. SHIVAS**
TD, MD, FRCSE, DPH, FRC Path
*formerly Senior Lecturer in Pathology*
*University of Edinburgh*

**EDINBURGH:**
at the University Press

© Andrew A. Shivas 1988
Edinburgh University Press
22 George Square, Edinburgh

Set in Itek Baskerville by
Waverley Graphics Ltd, Edinburgh and
printed in Great Britain by
Redwood Burn Ltd, Trowbridge

British Library Cataloguing
    in Publication Data
Shivas, Andrew A. (Andrew Armitage)
    The art of tympanist and drummer.—2nd ed.
    rev. and enlarged
    1. Drum playing—Manuals .
    I. Title
    789'.1
    ISBN 0 85224 574 2

# CONTENTS

# LIST OF ILLUSTRATIONS

# FOREWORD

DURING HIS undergraduate days, it was generally understood that when Andrew Shivas was not engaged in the study of medicine he would almost certainly be found playing some instrument. His search for enlarged instrumental experience led to our first meeting, at which I was at once impressed by the personal charm of this extraordinarily resourceful student, by his vitality, and by the particular manner, blended of delight and serious purpose, in which he approached the study of music.

Entering the University Orchestra, Andrew Shivas soon made the percussion department his own concern, with the tympani as the object of special affection. Here again, in all the work for which he made himself responsible the particular manner of approach was evident.

A particular manner is one of the evidences of style, and the particularity is largely one of adaptability; hence Parry's definition 'In art the most perfect style is that which is most perfectly adapted to all the conditions of presentment.' Throughout the fifteen years of my association with him, I have observed with ever-increasing appreciation the author's persistent and conspicuously successful adaptation of his style to the nature and aptitudes of his instrument, to its music, to consequent technical demands, and indeed to all the conditions of presentment.

In his orchestral activities Dr Shivas has constantly communicated his enthusiasm, engendering a ready response, and freely given of his artistic gains. While steadily improving his own technical and musical command, he has generously imparted to others so much of his knowledge as they have been able profitably to use. Of him it can be truly said 'Gladly would he learn and gladly teach.'

Now Dr Shivas offers the fruits of his study to a wider public. I anticipate that by so doing he will greatly increase the already considerable value of his contribution to orchestral playing, and in particular to that of the percussion department.

WILLAN SWAINSON

# PREFACE

THE OBJECT of this little book is to teach its readers the technique of tympani and percussion playing without the aid of a 'live' instructor. It is, of course, true that no practical skill can be fully imparted by the written or even spoken word. Demonstration to and *practice* by the pupil are essentials. Nevertheless, books on all forms of practical pursuits from bricklaying to badminton, watch-making to weight-lifting have appeared in recent years and their continued popularity is proof of their value. By no means a substitute for 'live' tuition they are much better than no tuition at all.

The musician, however, amateur or professional, appears to have been largely neglected. Books have from time to time appeared, generally dealing with the piano or members of the string family and a few have instructed players of other instruments in the special techniques of the dance band. Books designed simply to teach the novice to play his instrument remain few, with the percussion department perhaps more neglected than any other, despite the great numbers of young players in Boy Scout, Boys' Brigade, Cadet Force and similar bands, not to mention pipe bands, brass and military bands and amateur orchestras of all kinds.

There are on the market for every conceivable instrument books erroneously labelled 'tutors'. With rare exceptions they do not teach but consist chiefly of large numbers of valuable exercises. The novice is told *what* to do but given little or no advice on *how* to do it. My aim here is not to replace but to supplement these useful 'tutors' and provide so far as possible the missing teaching element. I am myself 'self taught' and therefore well aware of the questions that crop up in the minds of beginners learning only from books. The methods set out here are the outcome of twenty years of enthusiastic playing in every type of musical ensemble from 'Dixieland' jazz band and Scottish pipe band to symphony orchestra, together with some ten years teaching experience. The scientific method has been applied to the problem of finding the best technique for every aspect of the drummer's work.

The professional player guards jealously the 'tricks of the trade' and while I believe that most of these are laid bare in the following pages, they have been established by independent experiment; there is no breach of confidence.

Nevertheless, I should like to express my sincere thanks to Mr Raymond Gillies and Mr James M'Geachie of the Scottish National Orchestra, who, though never acting as teachers in the accepted sense, have given me the benefit over a period of many years of their thorough understanding and long experience of the whole range of problems considered in this book, of which they have read the manuscript. But for their friendship, encouragement and fine musical example it would never have been written. I have much pleasure also in acknowledging my indebtedness to Mr James Bradshaw, tympanist of the Philharmonia Orchestra, for the enthusiasm with which he gave up his time to discuss with me the essential principles of my thesis, and for his support of them. The manuscript was also read by Mr John Dalby, Music Organizer to Aberdeen City Education Department and Assistant Director of the National Youth Orchestra; he made many valuable suggestions which have improved the teaching ability of the book. The photographs are the work of my colleague Mr R. Drummond and there is no doubt that they contribute a major part of whatever value the book may have. From Mr Swainson, who has undertaken the awkward task of providing a foreword, I have learned most of what I know about music and, like all who have been privileged to play for him, owe him an enormous debt of gratitude.

Finally, I must thank my wife for much general help, patience and understanding during the writing, and my mother who typed the manuscript from my handwriting—a feat for which no praise can be too great.

# PREFACE TO THE SECOND EDITION

IN WRITING a preface for this edition my first duty is to apologise to the many people who have requested it since the first edition went out of print.

During a busy medical life involving much teaching, such time as I could find for authorship had of necessity to be devoted to medical literature. Limited time for music was best devoted to playing (happily in the same wide range of ensembles as previously) and some teaching. Now, however, in semi-retirement, the opportunity for a full revision and up-dating presents itself. Changes which have occurred in both instruments and technique have meant substantial additions to the original text, of which, however, a great deal has been retained because the demand for 'period' instruments in 'authentic' performances of earlier music seems likely to increase. The aim of the book remains the same—to teach the reader by the written word only, so far as that is possible. But whereas the original text was aimed very largely at the beginner, it seemed sensible in a complete revision to extend consideration to the more subtle problems of the more experienced player. A great stimulus has been the interest shown in professional circles. From Mr James Blades, that most famous player, teacher, author and broadcaster, over a period of many years, and more recently from Mr Nigel Shipway, leading London 'session' player and clinic tutor and Mr Michael Skinner, principal percussionist at Covent Garden and Professor of percussion at the Royal College of Music, I have received much encouragement. It is a special pleasure to express my most grateful thanks to them. I am much indebted to two former colleagues; Mr Max Mackenzie of the Royal College of Surgeons of Edinburgh produced the new illustrations and Dr Jeffrey Walsh and his staff of the Department of Physiology, University of Edinburgh made the electromyographic studies. To Mrs Helen Stein, who undertook the secretarial work must go the same praise as was accorded in the first edition to my mother. My handwriting has not improved in the intervening thirty years. Finally, it is a pleasure to thank Mr John Davidson and his staff at the Edinburgh University Press for their friendly expertise and helpfulness.

# INTRODUCTION

THE VALUE of a sound technique on the side drum cannot be overestimated. Not only is the instrument the most commonly used of all the percussion, in every type of ensemble except the symphony orchestra, but much of its technique is applicable to the beating of difficult passages on the tympani and xylophone, etc. The budding drummer should therefore *invariably start* by learning the side drum for once it has been mastered the beating technique of the other percussion will present no great difficulty and the student will be able to devote most of the attention to their special problems. Conversely, without such mastery no great skill will ever be attained on the tuned percussion. I feel it worthwhile to emphasize that experience of the tympani or xylophone will *not* help appreciably in learning the side drum. Only too often enthusiasts start with the tympani, on which with some knowledge of music and a minimum of technical ability they are soon able to render many straightforward parts, such as those of the Haydn symphonies, well enough for the average amateur orchestra. Later, to complete their equipment, they turn to the side drum, only to find its difficulties such that most give up the struggle.

From these remarks it will be evident that the beating technique of the side drum is much more difficult than that of the tuned percussion. This does not mean, of course, that the tympani are in general easier to play than the side drum for the tympanist has to face many complex musical problems which do not arise in side drumming.

The early stages of the side drum in particular require steady and intelligent application, but the result is well worth the effort for it should be remembered that every drummer is sooner or later called upon to play it and the more expert he or she may be on the other percussion, the more embarrassing is a poor performance on the side drum.

To sum up, a good side drummer, if he has reasonable musical ability, can usually become a good tympanist and xylophone player but a tympanist with no knowledge of the side drum is seldom a good performer and in learning the side drum has little if any advantage over a complete novice.

# 1. THE SIDE DRUM (SNARE DRUM)

## CHOICE OF INSTRUMENT

DESCRIPTIONS ABOUND elsewhere and only a few words of advice are included here. The 'separate tension' drum in which each skin or 'head' can be regulated independently is essential for the best results. Since the first edition of this book thirty years ago, plastic drumheads have been introduced, improved and are now almost universal. They have the great advantage of being little affected by atmospheric changes of temperature and humidity. This was a great problem with calf skin drumheads which are rarely seen today. Snares are usually of wire and, once set, require little adjusting. Gut snares or snares of silk strands wound with wire are occasionally used but need more frequent adjustment—especially with gut which is sensitive to atmospheric change.

In the tensioning of the heads, as in all matters of percussion playing, the ear is the ultimate guide, apart from the general rule that the snare head (the lower head on which the snares rest) must be slightly less tight than the batter (playing) head on which the sticks are used. The opposite view is held by some players but most find the above arrangement gives best results. To determine whether or not the snare head *is* at a lower tension the snare should be released and then each head tapped in turn with a stick or with the finger tip while the other hand is rested lightly on the head not being tapped to prevent its vibrating. The head at the lower tension will give the lower pitched sound. The heads can, of course, be roughly tested simply by pressing with the finger but small differences can hardly be appreciated in this way. Tension should be applied evenly and checked by tapping each head right round its circumference when the same pitch should be heard at all points. The adjustment of snares is a matter of experience and the ear is the only guide. The adjustment should be slackened until the snares are not acting at all and then gradually tightened while the batter head is tapped with a stick and the player listens until a crisp, staccato effect with no buzz is obtained. The novice learning from books only should take every opportunity of hearing and watching good players at as close quarters as possible. Seats in the organ gallery at symphony concerts are invaluable while much can be learned in a theatre from a seat in the orchestra stalls at the drummer's end of the 'pit'. Fortunately, the two alternatives are at opposite ends of the price range so that all pockets are catered for!

## STICKS

Sticks with a 'short taper' are most generally useful. This means that the shaft is of uniform thickness throughout most of its length and then tapers to the 'acorn'. Sticks with a 'long taper', i.e., tapering gradually throughout almost their whole length, facilitate the production of a long roll at all volumes up to about mezzoforte, but for greater volume they are useless as they simply do not have the weight where it is required—near the tip. Hickory is the best wood for side drum sticks and well worth the small extra cost. The weight of the stick should match the size of the drum. Side drums come in a variety of dimensions, the commonest for indoor playing being 14 inches in diameter and 5 or 6 inches in depth. For outdoor (military or military style) playing, or for greater power in a large orchestra, a larger drum is usual. It will be considerably deeper and often an inch wider. Such a drum, for best results, requires heavier sticks and a slightly more 'open' roll. This term is explained later.

## PLAYING POSITION

The photographs (figures 1 and 2) will give better instruction on this than any printed directions but a few supplementary remarks may be helpful. The standing position is usual in symphony orchestras and military bands, the sitting position in other ensembles. The player should stand or sit *upright* and avoid bending over or looking down at the instrument which may with advantage be canted at a greater angle for the standing position. When seated he should not lean back in the chair; the arms and wrists have more freedom of action if the back is kept straight and slightly away from the back of the chair. Apart from this, however, the *whole body should be relaxed*.

## GRIP FOR THE SIDE DRUM STICKS (figures 3-6)

Before considering this very important subject it will be as well to answer two questions that crop up repeatedly in the minds of beginners. 'Why must the left stick be held in such an awkward way, and is there any good reason why both sticks should not be held by the comfortable grip used for the right stick?' The answer to these questions is that side drumming has developed on a drum carried by the player on a sling over his right shoulder. This means that the instrument is very close to the body and hangs at an angle because it is impossible to march with a horizontal drum—or at any rate very

3

Figure 2. Sitting position for the side drum. This shows the alternative method of playing with the sticks on diametrically opposite points of the head. Note again that the 'playing spots' are equidistant from the rim.

Figure 1. Standing position for the side drum. Note that the tips of the sticks are close together, but equidistant from the rim to ensure as great uniformity of tone as possible.

4

painful. The type of grip which has been evolved for the left hand is the only one allowing the stick to be brought comfortably into the playing position. Regarding the second question, there is no theoretical reason why both sticks should not be held in the same way. Indeed, as this would be much nearer the technique used on the tuned percussion it might be argued that it should lead to better all-round performance. A player, however, must be assured that he will never have to play anything but a drum on a stand. The normal technique is hallowed by time and tradition and I feel sure that a player who had no command of it would tend to feel 'not quite a drummer'—especially if he were ever asked to play a drum hung over his shoulder on a sling. The student should therefore learn the traditional method first. He may later decide to change; it is not a difficult change to make. Some modern techniques of drum-kit playing are facilitated by the 'matched grip', as it has become known. For best results over the whole range of side drumming it is probably true to say that some facility is required with both techniques and individual players must decide for themselves which should have priority, bearing in mind the points made above.

## GENERAL REMARKS

It is important to realize that the action of a side drum-stick is closely similar to that of a lever and accordingly the aim in taking a grip is to hold the stick as far as possible *at a single point*, as if it were balanced on a knife-edge, so that when the tip of it strikes the drum head the elastic recoil of the head will throw it back with the greatest possible freedom. This means for practical purposes that each stick must be held by the absolute minimum which is, of course, two fingers. In the right hand the tip of the thumb and the forefinger are used with the stick as the *first* joint of the forefinger and the thumb pressed onto the shaft, as shown in the photograph. In the left hand the essential grip is between the *side* of the thumb and the base of the left index finger. The photographs will make all this clearer but the precise point on the stick at which the grip is taken must be found by trial and error as it varies slightly with every pair of sticks. The right spot is recognized by the fact that when gripped there the stick, if allowed just to *fall* onto the drum or a table top or similar surface, bounces back several times with ease and reasonable force. If the grip is too near the butt the stick will scarcely rebound at all, if too near the middle it will rebound slowly and rather 'lazily' and the subsequent bounces will be very weak. Experience will quickly show the ideal spot and needless to say it is the same for both sticks— unless they are not a pair, something to be avoided at all costs.

Having established the idea of the 'fulcrum' or 'balance point' the grip for each hand can be completed. In the left hand the ring

5

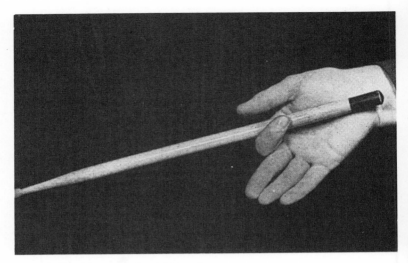

Figure 3. The fulcrum for the right hand.

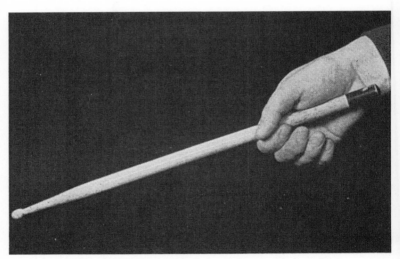

Figure 4. The complete grip for the right hand. Note that only the thumb and index finger actually *grip* the stick.

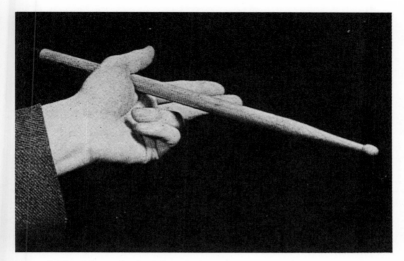

Figure 5. The fulcrum for the left hand.

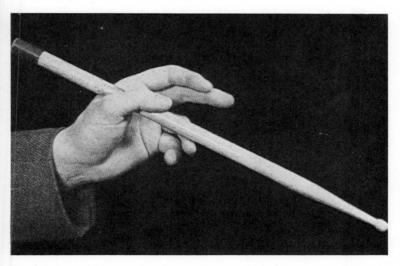

Figure 6. The complete grip for the left hand. Note that the index and middle fingers do *not* touch the stick.

and little fingers and curled round so that the stick lies on the ring finger just beyond the last joint. The thumb is bent downwards along the shaft of the stick and the index and middle fingers are held *in the air* as illustrated. They should not touch the stick. I know that some schools of thought believe that the fingers should rest on the stick but I am convinced that better control is ultimately gained if they do not. For completion of the right hand grip the three unoccupied fingers simply fall naturally into position alongside the index finger but do *not* touch the stick. The hand is turned over, palm down. Both elbows should be held slightly away from the sides. Again it must be stressed that these are not hard and fast rules and probably no two players use an exactly identical grip. Nevertheless, the grip described should be copied as closely as possible to ensure correct principles in the style eventually formed by the student, who must not be discouraged by the feeling that the left stick may fly out of his hand at any moment. This unpleasant sensation gradually disappears with experience. The ideal grip is always *firm*—but *relaxed*—never rigid or tense. There exist ethnic differences of left hand grip, the one illustrated and described being traditionally Scots, as used by the pipe band drummers. The Austrians use the same technique and it can be seen in the Vienna Philharmonic Orchestra! The English, Germans and Americans favour a left hand grip in which the index and middle fingers are curled round the stick and the wrist action is more twisting in movement. The French have yet another approach. Without being unduly nationalistic I think it may be said that the high quality of Scottish side drum technique is generally acknowledged. Before leaving the subject of ethnic differences, it should perhaps be noted that in recent years the American term 'snare drum' has become much more used than formerly.

### METHOD OF BEATING

As a preliminary, a point of anatomy should be explained. For practical purposes 'the muscles of the wrist' do not exist. In side drumming nearly all the movement takes place at the wrist, but the *power* comes from the forearms where a powerful group of muscles are situated and connected by long tendons to the hand and fingers. There are, of course, muscles in the hand itself, especially in relation to the thumb, but these serve in drumming chiefly to control the position of the sticks though in certain types of rapid playing they can give valuable help to the forearm muscles. The wrist must be regarded simply as a hinge at which the main movements of percussion playing occur.

## SINGLE STROKES

We come now to the actual striking of the drum and the student's first task is that of learning to produce *as nearly as possible* the same sound from a stroke with either stick. An exactly identical sound can never be achieved, for two reasons. Firstly, no two sticks are identical and if each is used in turn on the same spot on the drum head with equal force (even if the same hand is used to ensure this) two distinctly different sounds will result. Secondly, and more important, a drum head is prepared from an animal skin and no two parts of it are quite alike. In other words, if the head is struck in several different places with the same stick and with equal force, each place will yield its own particular note, different in quality from that of any other place on the head. It might thus appear that the task we have just set is impossible and in theory this is so, but fortunately, for practical purposes it can be accomplished because these differences are in *quality* only and though readily heard by the player they are scarcely perceptible to the listener some little distance away. It is important, however, for the student to know this as he might otherwise feel that his labours to beat equally with both hands were completely in vain. What he must produce is equality of *volume*, not uniformity of quality, though this too should always be aimed at as far as possible and the methods to be followed will be described later once the essential technique of making the strokes has been described. It will be obvious that the above instructions relate to calf skin drumheads, but they have been retained because a drum fitted with these may still be encountered occasionally. Further, while with plastic heads the variations in quality within a head are much less, the problem is by no means completely eliminated.

The development of equal ability with both hands is one of the fundamentals of percussion technique and is perhaps more difficult on the side drum than on tuned percussion. The right hand, generally the stronger and holding the stick in a natural way is opposed by the left and usually weaker hand holding the stick in a much less natural manner. I doubt whether any amount of practice will make the hands truly equal in ability but the weak hand can always be improved sufficiently for all practical needs. A naturally left-handed individual who has been taught to write with the right hand has, I believe, the best chance of achieving real equality of ability.

The actual stroke may be quite aptly likened to the action in cracking a whip. The tip of the stick is held about an inch above the drum head and the stick is flicked *upwards* and then 'cracked' downwards till it strikes the head, which will, by its elasticity, throw the stick back again in an upward direction. The whole movement is made *as one* and as the stick is thrown back after striking the head it is so to speak caught and held steady to prevent a second and subsequent 'bounce' on the drum. The points on the head on which the two sticks beat must be *equidistant* from the rim in order to obtain as nearly as possible the same tone from each stick. The importance of this will be immediately obvious if the player strikes the drum near the rim and then successively *with the same force*, inwards until the centre of the head is reached where a rather 'explosive' quality is obtained. The batter head, then, should be thought of as a series of concentric circles rather like a target, and the playing spots must *always lie on the same circle*. They may be close together or diametrically opposite (see illustrations) but if the latter position is adopted care should be taken to have them exactly opposite each other so that each is equidistant from the underlying snare. I personally like to play with the sticks immediately above each end of the snare but many players prefer to play at the ends of a diameter drawn at right angles to the snare, i.e., as far away from the ends of the snare as possible. It is largely a matter of taste but the first method gives more response from the snare in quiet passages. In general, such passages should be beaten near the rim and the sticks brought gradually nearer the centre of the head as increased volume is required. As already explained, however, whatever volume is in use the beating points must always be equidistant from the rim. The elastic recoil of the head diminishes towards the centre and so this part is not used for general purposes but only for a very loud fortussimo or a special effect where the 'explosive' tone quality already mentioned is suitable.

To begin with, the student should make single beats at an average march tempo and moderate volume. The left hand (in right-handed players) will tend to be weaker and must constantly be exerted more than the right to obtain evenness, remembering that the vital point is to achieve the same *amount* of sound from each stick. As already described, the quality will vary slightly but this is not readily perceptible to an audience. *It is essential to listen intently to every beat.* As skill advances the speed of the single strokes should be increased to about double the march tempo. At this speed it will be found that no conscious 'upward flick' is made for each stroke; its place is taken by the rebound from the *previous* beat so that the process as a whole is converted into what might be thought of as a 'chain' of beats rather than a succession of isolated 'links'. As a general rule, the student should *not* watch the sticks but look straight in front. In the earliest stages of any new rudiment or exercise it is permissible to watch the sticks but as soon as any degree of competence is achieved he should look to the front, remembering that in a band or orchestra there are music and conductor to be watched, making it essential to be able to play without looking at the instrument. A useful method however, is that of practising before a large mirror. This will immediately show any awkward or incorrect developments in stance, grip or beating technique by comparison with the photographs in the book and what the student can see for himself at concerts, etc.

Having brought single stroke technique up to the level just described, further study should be postponed until the essential rudiments described below have been at least moderately mastered.

## THE LONG ROLL

In the making of a single stroke, the importance of catching the stick after it has struck the drum *just once* was stressed. The production of the long roll requires just the opposite, and this very divergence is the basis of the difficulty of side drum technique as compared with the technique of the tuned percussion.

Correspondingly, however, once mastered, it imparts a degree of versatility which makes the production of all types of stroke on the tuned percussion relatively simple.

If the drum is struck as described for 'single stroke' but *without* the final movement of 'catching the stick', it will, having struck once, fall back on the head only to rebound yet again and again, the beats becoming progressively weaker and closer together till what amounts to a very short diminuendo roll completes the process. It will be evident then, that if this action is carried out by one hand after the other, continuously, and the interval between the initial wrist stroke is gradually decreased, something which at least approaches a long roll will result. Of course, as the interval between the strokes is decreased each stick will strike before the short 'crush roll' (as it is known) produced by its predecessor has died away, and this is what converts a series of isolated 'crush rolls' gradually into a more or less continuous note. Further, the rate of the 'crush' strokes (i.e., the individual bounces made by each stick) can be increased (known as 'closing the roll') by pressure on the right stick *upwards* with the tip of the right index finger and on the left stick *downwards* with the left thumb, the finger and thumb acting in the same way as a 'return spring' in a mechanical leverage system.

Due to the slope of the drum, the head of the left stick will tend, during each 'crush' roll to move 'downhill', so to speak, towards the centre of the head, and so the path of the head of the stick becomes an ellipse. This is advantageous as it helps to keep up the volume right to the end of the 'crush', since a light stroke near the centre, as the student has probably already discovered, produces more volume than a stroke of equal force near the rim. Of course, the movement must be imitated by the right stick, and here, as the head of the stick has to travel 'uphill' the player must deliberately impart the elliptical movement and move the head of the stick upwards towards the centre. The student using a 'matched grip' will, of course, find this unnecessary as the drum will be horizontal. The whole process helps to 'even up' the roll. The beginner should practise over the same range of speeds as given for 'single stroke' and should not attempt a faster roll until absolute evenness has been achieved with both hands. As before it will be necessary to exert the weaker hand more, and some time will generally be required to get this crush roll to a reasonable standard, but the *importance of doing so cannot be over-estimated*, and the single stroke and long roll should be practised daily, to the standards mentioned before proceeding further.

### THE RUDIMENTARY ROLL

At this stage it may be prudent to reassure drummers of the military school who have not already consigned the book to the fire, that there is no intention to exclude or even underestimate the value of the traditional development of the roll with which we shall now deal. The essentials of the true rudimentary or 'daddy-mummy' roll will be found in every tutor, but the instructions for its execution are often meagre. The student is told to strike *twice* with each stick in turn, commencing with the left and, keeping the beats exactly equal in strength, to increase their speed to a rapid pace 'when a roll will result'.

This evolution, as many readers will already be aware, is not merely difficult; it is impossible—in the manner described. The player *begins* by beating two separate strokes with each hand—not one stroke followed by a bounce but two individual and distinct beats, but as the speed increases, he changes over *imperceptibly* to beating only one stroke and allowing just *one* bounce or 'after-stroke' to occur (in the manner of beginning a crush roll) and then arrests the stick. The secret lies in being able to *play more rapidly using two individual beats* than the *slowest speed* at which the beats can be delivered evenly using the *single beat-and-after-stroke technique*.

This means that at an 'in-between' speed, the player can get a steady succession of beats by *either* method and so can make the change over without the slightest hesitation, faltering or unevenness. The other difficulty is in getting a good 'afterstroke' equal in strength to the original beat. This might at first seem impossible, but if the tip of the right index finger and the left thumb are used to flick the stick down again (with the same action as 'closing' the crush roll) after it has rebounded from the initial stroke, an afterstroke of equal or *even greater* force than the initial stroke, can be obtained. Of course, a

12

true rudimentary roll can only be 'closed' by increasing the speed of the *hands* (as each stick must make only one bounce) and to get a musically satisfactory effect, very great activity indeed is required.

In performance, however, a certain amount of 'crushing' is always introduced and so, from the practical standpoint there is little difference between the rudimentary and the crush roll, other than in their development. The ability to 'work up' a rudimentary roll is, however, of enormous value because of the facility in technique which it gives, and the player who masters it will never be 'caught out' on a rapid passage with an accelerando which has become too fast for single strokes. Further, a very loud roll can be achieved by only one method—that of using a near rudimentary roll (with little crushing) and at the greatest possible speed (consistent with evenness) almost in the centre of the head.

The rudimentary roll, therefore, is strongly recommended as part of the daily practice of every drummer as soon as a reasonable 'crush roll' can be produced.

It is important to note that every roll, of whatever type, should be started with a firm attack and finished with a *sharp, single stroke*. This is a general principle, especially for the beginner. However, depending on the musical context, there are occasions when a roll must start so quietly as to 'appear from nothing' or end so quietly as simply to vanish. In such instances, clearly, initial attack or firm final stroke must be omitted.

The speed of the beating should be entirely unrelated to the speed of the music. Indeed, the player should frequently practise in private until he can carry on a conversation and still continue rolling. By doing this he will learn to give his entire attention when in the orchestra to the music and conductor and will be quite unperturbed by variations in tempo. A useful addition to the technique is the 'triplet roll'. This simply means that the roll is beaten with an accent as if playing groups of triplets thus:

At first the accent should be played quite firmly, but later gradually reduced until the player hardly does more than think of it, and the hands, when rolling, settle down automatically into the triplet rhythm. It is considered that this method of roll has definite advantages musically for the following reasons.

A drum roll is supposed ideally to sound as a continuous note, but, as it is in fact a succession of beats played by two hands alternating it tends, even with the most skilled players, to acquire a 'see-saw' quality.

13

If a triplet accent be added to this 'see-saw', two phase wave motion, a three phase motion is superimposed on it, and the effect tends to be so complex as to confuse the ear of a listener by 'fogging' the 'see-saw' periodicity, so that, if well practised and carefully played, an effect closer to a sustained note is achieved. A further refinement of this device is that of varying the speed of the strokes. The listener probably requires three or four seconds before the periodicity of beating is recognised and if at that point the rate of the strokes is altered a further few seconds will pass before recognition can again occur. Consequently, such variation can postpone for as long as is required the ability of the listener to hear the 'see-saw'. When using this technique, however, it is vital not to allow the *volume* to vary, getting louder as the beating speeds up, quieter as the strokes become slower. It should also be realised that a roll in which the 'see-saw' is perceptible, by suggesting the ticking away of the seconds, may be used to good effect where an atmosphere of suspense or tension is required rather than that of a heraldic occasion such as the National Anthem.

### PIANO ROLL

It has already been said that piano passages should in general be played near the rim, and this holds good for the piano roll. A long-sustained piano roll evenly executed is probably the most difficult technical accomplishment in the whole of percussion playing.

A mezzoforte roll, if carried out to the edge of the drum, will give a reasonable piano roll, but to obtain a still quieter roll great skill is required, especially with the left hand. The ideal technique probably varies from player to player, but in general, active force in the strokes must be nearly stopped and the sticks allowed rather to fall gently onto the head, the right index finger and the left thumb imparting the required degree of 'crush' for a close roll. The speed of beating for best results will vary from player to player. Each must experiment. It is a technique that takes much practice over a long time to acquire, in most cases, and a difficulty is that the amount of playing available in a 'straight' orchestra is woefully inadequate to maintain the necessary standard of technique.

In my experience, the 'music hall' drummer generally performs it better for this reason than a symphony orchestra player. The following is a useful exercise:

It should eventually be played *continuously* (i.e., without any break) for several minutes on end.

### SPEED OF BEATING OF ROLLS

No rule can be laid down as individual players will achieve their best results at differing speeds, but as a general guide, a mezzoforte or forte roll should be beaten about the speed shown below:

Each note, of course, indicates a wrist stroke, not one individual bounce of the stick head on the drum i.e., the speed indicated is that at which the *hands* are moving.

### SHORT ROLLS

These rudiments, shown in alarming numbers in many tutors, are an important and characteristic part of side drum technique but present no difficulties once the long roll has been mastered, since they are merely short sections of long roll. They range in the tutors from five to fifteen or more strokes with an entirely needless complexity and are usually shown as below. Here the much-used seven stroke roll is taken as an example:

i.e. three 'daddy-mummy' strokes and a single one to finish (as in the long roll).

In practice, 'crush' beats are used instead of the rudimentary 'daddy-mummy'. This would be used to play the short rolls in a rhythm such as this in march time.

Needless to say, if this were taken much slower a seven-stroke roll would be too short and a nine or eleven-stroke roll would be required. While practice of the five, seven and nine-stroke rolls is recommended for the sake of familiarity and facility, the others may be ignored. One simply rolls for the period required, whether it be a quaver, a minim or several bars. It is useful to practise the short rolls with the beating reversed so as to be able to begin with either hand. A player who can only start a roll, whether it be short or long, with one hand will eventually land in difficulties such as having to play two notes in succession—possibly in a quick passage, with one hand in order to have the other hand ready to begin a roll. Good rolls are the hall mark of a competent side drummer—the short rolls crisp, attacked and finished decisively and the long rolls even and smooth. It is impossible to devote too much time to the practice of the rolls—especially the long roll.

### THE PARADIDDLE

This beat and its modifications loom large in military playing where it originated, and most 'tutors' include it. It has been said that a player who can read his part does not need the paradiddle which was essentially a means of keeping count easily of a large number of short notes when a player had to memorize his beatings. This is true, but the paradiddle is a most valuable exercise, and, in addition, can often be used to negotiate awkward passages on the xylophone or tympani. It is therefore commended to the student for practice and is shown below:

It should be practised slowly at first, and the speed gradually increased, ensuring that every beat has the *same force* and *duration*. As speed is gained the two 'doubled' semiquavers in each group should be played by the 'after-stroke' method as in the 'daddy-mummy' roll and the exercise 'worked up' to the speed of an open roll. It is much used at this speed by the modern school of pipeband drumming, but it must be confessed that great practice is required at these higher speeds to avoid a slight accent at the beginning of each group.

### EMBELLISHMENTS

These are very important and much used in side drumming. They are relatively simple but must be neatly and accurately beaten. The three important ones are the flam, the drag and the ruff.

### THE FLAM

16

The grace note should be played lightly, but audibly; as near the principal note as possible, but not so near as to lose its identity. Listening to good players will give the best advice.

### THE DRAG

The same general remarks apply but it is impractical to attempt to ensure that precisely two bounces occur. In effect, a very short crush roll is played very lightly.

### THE RUFF

This is best beaten as marked and a good deal of practice is required to get the three grace notes rapid enough without being too loud. When beaten in this way, however, it has a highly distinctive and forceful character, quite different from the drag. Analysis of what, precisely, is happening at the higher speeds which *must* be attained if the correct effect is to be achieved will be amply repaid; it is the secret of success. It will be obvious that each hand makes two strokes. At a high speed these can only be delivered by the afterstroke (daddy-mummy) technique and what is required is that the double strokes are 'staggered', i.e. the first stroke of the right hand pair is delivered immediately the left stick has made its initial stroke. The final accent required to give the principal note its proper emphasis is achieved by a flick upwards with the tip of the right index finger which of course brings the stick sharply down on to the drumhead. When facility has been gained and the beating is reversed this action is carried out by the left thumb flicking downwards.

All embellishments should be practised with the beating reversed until they can be played fluently commencing with either hand.

### SINGLE STROKE TECHNIQUE

The elements of this have already been considered but once the foregoing techniques have been mastered, further practice of single-stroke beating will be of great value in consolidating a sound technique. It should be worked up at least to the speed shown below:

**17**

Absolute evenness should be aimed at, with no trace of any accent, so that when played at speed the exercise amounts to a 'single stroke roll'. As with the long roll, sustained periods of practice from *ppp* to *fff* and returning to *ppp* will be found very beneficial, and, in conjunction with the practice described earlier, should eventually leave the player undismayed by any orchestral part, so far as its technical demands are concerned.

### PRACTICE

In the early stages, short periods of fifteen to twenty minutes are best as the muscles fatigue quickly. There is no harm in doing more than one such spell in the day, if time allows, so long as there is an interval of an hour or two to allow the muscles to recover.

During the practice itself, short rests should be taken as soon as fatigue—first noticeable as a sensation of 'tightness' in the forearm—occurs.

Regularity is of the greatest importance. More will be achieved by a regular half-hour of practice daily than by occasional spasms of several hours in the same day.

A system of some kind, too, goes far to get the best out of the time available for practice. For example, in a practice period of half-an-hour one might do fifteen minutes at the long roll, including, of course, the rudimentary roll 'worked up' from 'daddy-mummy', followed by ten minutes at the short rolls and paradiddle, and a final five minutes perhaps devoted to the side drum part of some particular work or works in which the instrument is prominently featured.

This last type of practice is valuable in that one has a chance of getting to know the difficulties of parts in privacy, which is beneficial for the nerves when at some future time the same part turns up at rehearsal.

If, in commencing either practice or playing in the orchestra, the wrists should feel stiff and the muscles cramped, as may readily happen after lifting heavy weights or even after a long spell of writing, a useful exercise is to grasp each side drum stick about the middle with the fist clenched around it and twist it either way as far as possible at a moderate speed until exhaustion is felt. The muscles should then be rested for a few minutes and practice recommenced. It will generally be found that this will have dispelled any muscular spasm.

It is well to bear in mind that to make anything 'safe' for the concert hall it must be practised sufficiently to allow a margin for 'nerves', from which few players are entirely immune. It is not enough *just* to be able to manage a passage in practice. It must be worked at until it can still be played even if the player is almost shaking with fright. These remarks apply, of course, to almost any instrument, but the side drum is an instrument of peculiarly subtle technique to which 'nerves' or want of practice are very destructive. For this reason it is wise to practise fairly frequently even after the instrument has been reasonably mastered. Two years may easily be required to repair the effects of six months neglect.

### NOISE ABATEMENT

A few words on this subject by way of conclusion may preserve the drummer from much domestic trouble. Naturally, it is advisable to do, say, at least half one's practice on the drum under normal playing conditions, but for the remainder several devices may be used with great effect in reducing the volume of sound but with no notable loss of training value.

Firstly, the snares may be put 'off' and a book or large cloth or rubber pad laid on the batter head. This will slide down the drum and leave exposed the opposite side of the batter head. This part may then be played upon with very little noise. Secondly, various 'practice pads' are obtainable, consisting generally of a rubber slab mounted in a wooden holder which is set at an angle. Many are quite useless and only a very good one, heavily made and giving a good 'rebound' is recommended. A good alternative is to play on the metal lid of a wide-mouthed screwtop jar of the type in which anything from honey to pickles is marketed. Some experiment may be needed to get a good one with plenty of spring, but the research is worthwhile as they deteriorate only very slowly. Lastly, a certain amount of practice can be done by playing on one's own thigh, sitting with legs crossed. There is, of course, no rebound at all and this method can only be used for 'single stroke' work. Should it become unduly painful a cushion or similar object may be used.

## 2. THE TYMPANI

THE FACT that this small book has no pretensions to completeness has already been mentioned, but it is perhaps wise to stress it again at this point. Tympani playing can, and has, provided many musicians with a life-time of study and what follows here is to be regarded only as a bare outline, an indication to the student of the directions along which to further his own studies. As with the side drum, material which is readily available in 'tutors' or from other sources such as orchestration text-books, has been omitted for the sake of brevity and the resulting economy. This section of the book has nevertheless been considerably expanded, of necessity, to accommodate the many changes which have taken place since the first edition. At that time pedal tympani were a rarity hardly seen outside the professional symphony orchestra; plastic drumheads did not exist. Tuition in the percussion instruments was difficult— even impossible—to obtain except in the largest cities, and colleges of music had not thought it necessary to cater for the percussionist. There was no examination structure leading to diplomas, and teaching within a school was rarely available unless for a military band or (in Scotland) a school pipe band, covering only side drum, bass and tenor drums. Indeed, it was the inaccessibility of teaching which led directly to the writing of this book.

The scene today, as many readers will know, is vastly different. It remains true, however, that availability of teaching falls far short of the ideal—a fact which has been a prime factor in prompting a second edition. Pedal tympani are in common use, fitted with plastic heads, and have greatly simplified many of the tuning problems of hand drum and calf drumheads. But other problems peculiar to the new instruments have arisen and require consideration. Many schools and amateur orchestras are, however, still equipped with hand drums fitted with calf heads, a situation likely to be long lasting due not only to the great expense of replacing them with pedal drums but also to the interest in them as so-called 'baroque tympani' in playing with other 'authentic instruments' in the performance of the appropriate repertoire of orchestral music of the earlier period. Accordingly, I have thought it best to retain all the instructional material on these instruments and, in any case, the principles of tympani playing are the same, irrespective of the type of instrument. A paradoxical situation exists. There are in many schools young players who have experience only of hand drums but who, on leaving school, will certainly meet with pedal drums. In other schools we find players taught entirely on pedal drums but who, sooner or later, will find themselves expected to play on hand drums—a much greater problem than that facing the first group trained on hand drums and later finding themselves behind pedal tympani, for reasons which will emerge later.

In recent years, both pedal and hand tympani have been produced with shells of fibreglass instead of the traditional copper. These are lighter in weight and do not dent, features very attractive in school use, especially as they are also lower in price. But they do not have the tone quality of copper bowls, the deficiency being particularly in the louder dynamics, when the quality of the ensemble sound suffers noticeably with a large orchestra. It is also worth noting that, even allowing for the economy of a fibreglass shell, the pedal drum remains a very expensive instrument.

Fundamentally, the side drummer is confronted with only one problem—the demarcation of rhythm.

The tympanist, on the other hand, is confronted with three—the demarcation of rhythm, the maintenance of determinate pitch, and, perhaps most difficult of all, the production of that elusive quality 'good tone'. Further, the first quality, rhythm, is in some measure antagonistic to the third, due to the particular character of the tympani with their large heads at low tension and big resonating chambers.

These features, in conjunction with properly-designed sticks, impart the characteristic 'booming' note and long reverberation of the tympani—the exact antithesis of the side drum and clearly not ideally suited to rhythm marking. The qualities of rhythm and tone are thus not complementary and occasionally, according to circumstances, one may have to be in some measure sacrificed for the other.

Tone may be gained at the expense of rhythm, and vice versa, but constant endeavour to achieve accuracy of pitch must *never* be relaxed. From the foregoing it will be obvious that technique cannot be sharply subdivided into beating, tuning and tone, for all are interdependent.

### THE STICKS

Paralleling the great changes in the instruments, a range of sticks, many of excellent quality, is now available from the best instrument dealers. The situation of thirty years ago, when it was extremely difficult, if not impossible, to buy good sticks, has been completely transformed. Yet some tympanists continue to make their own, perhaps because only in this way can the requirements (which vary with the individual) be precisely met. But it must be stressed that stick-making is not an easy craft and can be time-consuming. It is not likely to come easily to anyone who is not a reasonably good handyman. Tympani sticks are a very variable piece of equipment and most players can gradually acquire, by purchasing selectively, a range of sticks to suit their individual needs. The process may spread over years as only with steadily increasing experience and acuity of tone perception will the player come to know exactly what he wants in a particular type of stick—and how to use it.

The flexible cane shafts, once popular with many though not all British tympanists, are rarely seen today and a rigid shaft of hickory or similar wood is usual. Stiff cane is used by some makers. Heads are generally of two parts—an inner core and an outer cover of piano damper felt. The inner core is best made of an incompressible material such as cork. Felt is sometimes used but this is nearly always compressible and because the compression occurs as the stick strikes the drum, it results in a longer period of contact with the drumhead and, acting as a damper, impairs the tone as well as the attack. The effect is less with a very hard (or dense) felt for the core, but often there is little difference in consistence between the inner and outer felt. Cork and balsa wood have proved satisfactory as core material, but anything incompressible should give good results. We must now consider the traditional terms 'hard', 'medium' and 'soft' as descriptions of tympani sticks and look critically at their true meaning. What is really being described is the thickness of the outer cover of piano damper felt. This felt is purchased as a sheet but is not applied in this form to the stick. The sheet is split with the fingers into two thinner sheets. This gives a very 'fluffy' surface which goes to the *outside* of the stick head. A thick cover gives a 'soft' stick and a thin one a 'hard' stick but the terms only have meaning in relation to the force with which they are used, i.e. the dynamics of the music, something so variable as to make the terms 'hard' and 'soft' almost meaningless. A thinly covered ('hard') stick, if lightly used, will give a soft sound and conversely, a thickly covered ('soft') stick can give a hard quality of sound if used with sufficient force. Failure to grasp this principle results in some muddled thinking. It is not unusual, for instance, to see in print the advice to players to 'avoid rolling with hard sticks'. This advice is valid only for a loud roll; a piano roll may sound very satisfactory, the maximum acceptable dynamic varying with the thickness of the outer felt. Both the overall size and the weight of the stick head are important as well as the consistency and

22

thickness of the outer felt. To take an example, a small head will bring less felt into contact with the drum and so give a very 'clean' attack. Thus a small head which is also fairly heavy and thinly covered will give excellent single pianissimo or piano notes such as often form part of a solo for the drums. It will be evident that, with so many variable factors in their construction there exists an almost unlimited variety and a player's sticks are ultimately an expression of his individual musical taste. The main difficulty in making sticks is that of achieving a truly identical result in every one of a series, such that every pair really *are* an exact match. While in this, as in most things 'you get what you pay for' high price is not a guarantee of perfection and, if at all possible, a pair of sticks should be tried *on the tympani* before parting with the money! There are two further points. Variation between the two sticks of a pair can develop with use and in an extreme instance might demand recovering as the only remedy. Problems can also exist within a single stick, even when new. These result from the difficulty of sewing a cover with absolute uniformity of tension round the whole of its circumference. A lax point will give a softer, 'rounder' sound while a more highly tensioned spot will give a harder quality. If a pair of sticks are otherwise well matched it may be possible, by marking the shaft so that the hard or soft spot never strikes the drum, to continue their use, but it is a constant irritation and distraction and very much a last resort. What emerges from all this, in practical terms? Few pairs of sticks are identical in all respects and the player learns to 'phrase' his use of them to get the best effect, which may involve always using the same stick in the same hand. In addition, while in no way seeking to undermine the general rules of tympani technique, a skilful player will often tackle as much as possible of an important and exposed figuration with one stick, to give as near perfect uniformity of tone as may be possible. An unerring sense in the choice of such passages and the best use elsewhere of hand-to-hand beating with the occasional doubled beat or paradiddle as the 'phrasing' may require, is one of the cardinal points indicating a fine player. Closely allied to this, of course, is the selection of the sticks from his range for a given passage. Many are the occasions on which, ideally, sticks should be changed in the middle of a passage—frequently an impossibility. But of the two pairs of sticks in question, one may produce more shortcomings than the other. The best tympanist will always make the correct choice. It is largely such subtle nuances as these which, other things being equal, separate the very finest performers from those of just slightly less stature.

A very useful type of stick first introduced by Mr James Blades has a shaft of uniform thickness, almost as thick as a side drum stick and sometimes fitted with a hard collar at the butt end. Such sticks can be reversed for use on the side drum or even the xylophone and glockenspiel, and are valuable in theatre playing where the part often demands a change of instrument but allows no time for a change of stick! The 'balance' of these sticks feels at first a little strange but can soon become comfortable. The tone obtained from the 'keyboard' instruments is, of course, inferior in volume and quality to that produced by the proper beaters, but this is much preferable to missing some of the part completely. Finally, before leaving the subject of sticks, it has to be admitted that much of the subtlety described in the foregoing paragraphs will be imperceptible to all but a small proportion of listeners. Even among percussionists, only some will develop a sufficiently acute ear to distinguish these fine shades of tonal difference. Not all conductors can hear them, but the best ones always can, enabling them to appoint a tympanist to the best advantage of the orchestra. This knowledge is a great encouragement to tympanists, who might otherwise wonder whether their conscientious efforts to achieve the very finest results were lost on all but themselves and a few fellow tympanists!

### GRIP

The grip is the same for both hands (figures 7 and 8). The stick is mainly held by the thumb, index and middle fingers, the other fingers falling into a natural position. The stick lies on the last joint of the index finger and *second* joint of the middle finger. The thumb nails face straight upwards. In quiet playing most of the gripping is done by the thumb and the two fingers, and the mechanism is shown in the photographs. It is very important to have the index finger *in front* of the thumb so that it is available to act as a 'return spring' to get the stick up off the head after the stroke with the least possible delay. In heavy playing the whole hand except for the little finger participates in the grip and the thumb tends to slide forward, level with the index finger, unless it happens to be a very short thumb. This is of no consequence, however, and it is pulled back a little when the loud passage is over.

As with the side drum sticks, the ideal point at which the grip should be taken varies with each pair of sticks, being determined by the 'balance', which depends mainly on the weight of the head and the length of the shaft. Again, it can be found only by trial and error, but it may be said that a grip too near the 'butt' will hamper the player by the extra weight he has to move in beating, while one too near the head, conversely, will make the sticks light to handle but will therefore call for more work from the player in a loud passage. A small amount of practice will reveal the best point of grip for any pair of sticks and the illustrations will give a rough guide to begin with.

24

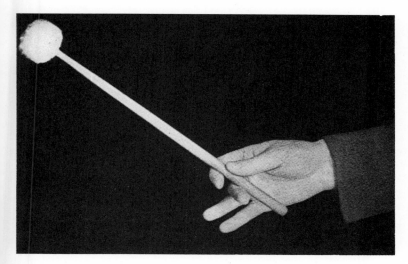

Figure 7. Fulcrum for the tympani stick. This is not strictly a fulcrum in the physical sense, as the three fingers cover a short length of the stick, but in practice the effect is similar and the term is retained for convenience.

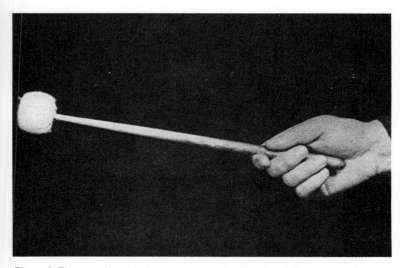

Figure 8. The complete grip for the tympani stick. The fourth finger may grip the stick in heavy playing, but *not* the little finger. The stick itself is 14 inches long with a hickory shaft which is almost rigid. This gives better control than a 'whippy' cane shaft and is better 'balanced'.

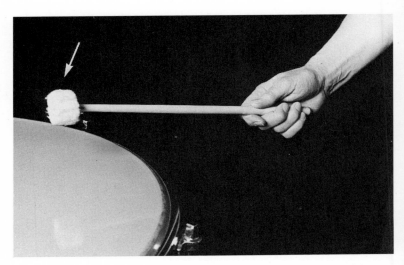

Figure 9. The downstroke, 'thumb uppermost' grip. This is the most powerful wrist stroke, using a combination of forearm muscle groups. Note the power-transmitting tendons above the wrist joint.

Figure 10. The upstroke, 'thumb uppermost' grip. Using the same muscles as the corresponding downstroke (Figure 9), this has considerable power and maximum 'elastic recoil' from the drum head.

Figure 11. The downstroke, 'palm down' grip. This has great power, using the flexor muscles, but is slightly less powerful than the downstroke with the 'thumb uppermost" grip.

Figure 12. The upstroke, 'palm down' grip. Using only the extensor muscles, this is a relatively weak action, giving a less effective recoil from the drum head. The difference is most obvious in piano or pianissimo strokes, when the drum head contributes little to the recoil.

There is an alternative grip for the tympani stick closely similar to that for the right hand side drum stick. It does not offer either the range of volume or tone given by the grip previously described and illustrated, because it utilises weaker muscle groups. In particular, in quiet rolls, because the recovery (upstroke) from the drumhead is slower there is more surface noise and more damping. This, especially with a rapid roll, gives a slightly muted and 'muttering' effect of a very exciting or 'threatening' quality. It can be used to very good effect where such an atmosphere has to be created—especially when a crescendo is also involved. If the other, and generally better, grip is used in such circumstances, a more 'musical' result is obtained but that is not the prime requirement, which should be subordinated to evocative 'effect'. A player thus ideally requires facility with both grips and most can achieve it. Occasional individuals find that they are comfortable only with one or the other. Both actions, with some explanation of their differences, are illustrated in figures 9-12.

### BEATING

As will already be obvious, the most important point in making the single stroke is that it must be as nearly as possible instantaneous. The general principles are just the same as in making the single stroke on the side drum with the notable exception that whereas on that instrument the rigidity of the stick and elasticity of the head can be relied upon to throw back the stick immediately its full weight has struck, this helpful process occurs only to a limited extent on the tympani. The head of the stick is relatively soft and does not tend to 'rebound' so readily, while the tension of the head is nearly always less than that of the side drum, and usually much less, so that it has less effect in 'throwing back' the stick after the stroke. It therefore follows that the player himself must provide the lightning 'recoil' of the stick after the blow and hence the action of the single stroke in tympani playing is even more like that of cracking a whip than in side drumming.

As always, the action is one of wrist and fingers only. The stick is 'flicked' upwards, brought down on the head and instantly 'flicked' back again. The movements are executed as a single whole so as to form just one smooth action with what can only be described as an elastic or springing quality.

Pressure *upwards* with the index finger as described earlier is vital, and when correctly done makes a great difference to the tone obtained, especially in piano rolls and strokes and an expert player can alter the amount of upward pressure to obtain subtle variations of tone. One should never have the sensation of playing 'through' the drum, as if driving nails into it, but rather a feeling of 'picking'

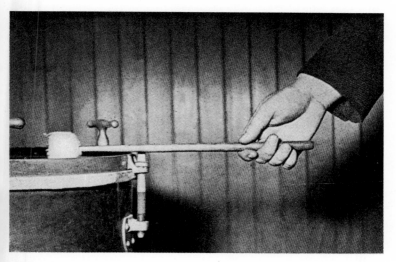

Figure 13. The correct angle for the stick in striking the drum. The shaft is nearly parallel with the drum head, having just sufficient angle to clear the rim.

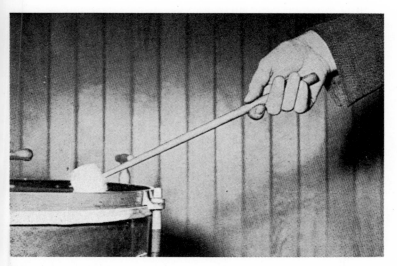

Figure 14. The *wrong* way. The fault shown here is deliberately exaggerated but minor degrees of it are common. It results in a 'glancing' blow, with impairment of tone and attack.

the notes off it. The roll, as every 'tutor' states, consists of a succession of *single strokes*. This constitutes the essential difference in beating technique between the tympani and side drum. In contrast with side drum technique, the use of alternate sticks is the almost invariable rule on the tympani. Even in rhythm playing the use of 'doubled' beats is to be recommended only in special circumstances which are discussed later.

The beginner must first learn to produce single strokes with absolute evenness of volume, and so far as possible, tone, just as with the side drum. The same difficulties will be encountered again. No two sticks will give exactly the same quality, nor any two places on the head, but if the side drum has been reasonably mastered these difficulties will be quite soon overcome so far as it is possible to overcome them. Again as with the side drum they can never be entirely conquered and the process of training the hands to attain evenness is never completed. Minor differences in quality, too, are apt to be more obvious on the tympani than on the side drum. For this reason the sticks should be used on as small an area as is consistent with ensuring that they do not collide. Where one is dealing with plastic tympani heads, however, there is a very important proviso. If a roll is played in the traditional fashion, with the heads of the sticks falling on a small area, there is relatively more surface noise than if the sticks are more widely separated, as in the illustrations (figures 15 and 16). The reasons for this are at present totally obscure; the effect certainly does not occur with calf heads. It gives a distinctly smoother roll, while a return to the usual 'beating spot', because of the greater surface noise, enhances the definition of rhythmic figures. It is therefore a feature of which every advantage should be taken. Another less important point about the plastic head is that better tone can be obtained a little nearer the centre of the drum than with a natural, calf head.

The selection of the 'beating spot' is of some importance as it affects the tone very considerably. Just inside the counter hoop, i.e. on the very edge of the head, a rather bright 'pinging' quality is obtained which lacks 'body' and 'depth' of tone and is suitable only for passages to which that tone is appropriate. As the sticks are moved gradually forward away from the edge of the head the 'brightness' is diminished and the fuller, 'deeper' tone which may be regarded as the characteristic quality of the tympani for general purposes is obtained. The best definition of the pitch is also obtained in this area. Beyond this, as the sticks approach still nearer to the centre of the head a dull 'thumping' quality appears and definition of the pitch is generally less good.

Once again this tone is suitable only for occasional special effects. It will be evident that in this matter of selection of the beating

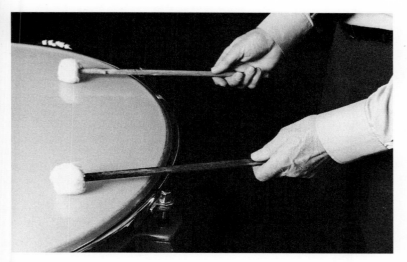

Figure 15. This shows the approximate degree of separation of the sticks to obtain minimum surface noise in a roll on a plastic head. The absence of tuning handles and counter hoop above the level of the head facilitates all types of execution.

Figure 16. The classical position for the sticks, which, with greater surface noise gives better definition of rythmic passages than if the position for the roll is used.

spot the player's good taste and artistic discretion are of great importance. Some writers have given measurements to indicate precisely how far from the edge it should be, but it is much better to be guided by the ear as no general rule is adequate. Quite apart from the range of tone the spot at which the best tone of any particular type is obtained varies with the size of the drum and, on a single drum, with the tension of the head, i.e. with the note that happens to be in use. In general if the head is at low tension a better quality will be obtained nearer the edge than if it is at high tension.

The student should make himself familiar with the tonal range of his drums while practising single strokes.

As proficiency is gained the rate of the single strokes should be gradually increased up to about the speed shown below.

At this speed it will be found that the individual beats lose their identity, chiefly due to the generous reverberations of the drum, resulting in a reasonably acceptable roll on any notes except those requiring the greatest tension, where rather more speed is required for even a passable roll. To the player himself, of course, the effect will not sound very satisfactory since he hears the actual surface noise of the beating very clearly and so does not get the impression of a continuous note. The surface noises, however, have little carrying power and a few yards from the drum the effect is that of a roll. This will probably come as a surprise to many readers but any who desire to put the matter to test need only stand beside the drum while another player beats at the speed indicated, and then walk away a distance of thirty feet or so, noting how the beats are 'smoothed out'.

Contrary to the impression of most learners it is neither necessary nor advisable to beat with the frenzy of one possessed to obtain a roll on the tympani. Speed can be useful, as will presently be discussed, but it is not vital. What *is* vital is *evenness*. Any inequality in the beating, especially if it is a regularity occurring one such as results from a weak left hand, ruins the effect even more easily than with the side drum roll.

It will be found that when rolling at this speed, or faster, the stick does show a certain tendency to 'rebound' like a side drum stick. The degree of rebound varies with the tension of the head, as might be expected, and increases with the speed and force of the beating. When it is felt it should be allowed full play as it does much to prevent fatigue. The player should feel that he merely 'flicks' the sticks at the top of the stroke, rather like bouncing a ball, and upward pressure with the index finger should be relaxed.

The action is thus one of wrist and fingers combined and the illustrations should again be carefully studied. Having struck the drum, the head is thrown back into the air and at the top of the stroke is flicked down again, chiefly by the fingers, only to bounce up again. The finger action should be developed in each hand separately by making an initial firm wrist-stroke and then attempting to 'keep the stick bouncing' *with the fingers only*, holding the wrist as nearly as possible motionless. The ring fingers should be used to assist the middle fingers. Naturally, the action only operates well when some force is used and this form of roll is less applicable in piano passages or indeed anything much less than mezzoforte in a normal symphony orchestra. For quiet passages the wrists must be relied on, though with experience it is possible to get some assistance from the fingers even in the quietest piano.

Similarly, for the heaviest fortissimo rolls, such as that which occurs ar the end of Tschaikowsky's *Romeo and Juliet* the finger technique alone will not give enough volume. The sticks must be gripped firmly, though not tensely, by all except the little fingers and the strokes made with sufficient force to give the required volume but with the utmost concentration to preserve correct action, obtain good tone and generally prevent the roll from degenerating into the frenzied and toneless hammering that is all too frequently seen and heard.

The thumb will automatically slide forward a little but this does not matter as in heavy playing the index finger merely grips instead of acting by upward pressure as a 'return spring'. This mechanism becomes superfluous once the stick begins to bounce back naturally from the heavier strokes. The whole movement should take place at the wrist, as always. It is neither necessary nor desirable to resort to the muscles of the upper arm and to beat from the elbow. Besides looking very laboured and ungainly such an action is under little control. It is essential that the sticks rise and fall *vertically* as otherwise a 'glancing' blow results and the period of contact of the stick with the drum head is prolonged, with resulting loss of tone.

Another important point is the *height of the hands* above the drum. This should be such that when the head of the stick strikes the drum the shaft is nearly parallel with the drum head.

The usual mistake is in having the drum too low so that, again, a 'glancing' blow result with some loss of tone.

### PLAYING POSITION

Since the question of position of the drums and player has been raised the more important aspects of this subject might now be discussed. Some of the finest performers play seated on a stool

33

similar to that used by the double-bass players; other equally fine exponents stand. Obviously, no general rule can be given but it is perhaps better to start with a standing position and experiment later with the sitting position if desired. A very tall player may find difficulty in getting the drums high enough to bring the hands comfortably to the proper playing position without his having to bend. Such a person should cultivate the sitting position unless he is naturally much more at ease standing, when the length of the sliding legs can always be specially increased to get the drums higher. Of course, even then, he would land in difficulty with any except his own instruments.

With pedal drums it is generally stated that the player should be seated, at least if much pedalling is required, as it is desirable that both feet should be available for the pedals. However, it must be remembered that a player who has to move between instruments, as in a concert band or light orchestras, say from xylophone to tympani, cannot play seated and the drums are therefore built to a height which is convenient for the standing position. Of course, only one or other foot is available for tuning. This may at first seem a great disadvantage but there are important qualifying points to be considered before coming to this conclusion. First, only an occasional work will require the use of both pedals more or less simultaneously. Secondly, a seat which will *safely* provide this facility is quite specialised, heavy and awkward to transport. It is of the type usually seen in the professional symphony orchestra and of very heavy construction with a very wide base incorporating a serrated ring against which the player can push to rotate the swivel seat, equipped with a strong backrest. This allows firm pressure on the pedals with either or both feet without risk of the seat moving.

The usual drum stool, which is all that will be available to most players, while quite adequate for sitting at a drum kit (its designed purpose) is unsatisfactory for the type of playing referred to above. It lacks a wide base, a backrest and heavy construction. Firm pressure on a pedal is liable to tip the stool backwards; firm pressure on two pedals is almost certain to do so. The risks are less with the 'balanced action' pedal of the American Ludwig drum but are very real with the Premier pedal which is by far the commoner of the two in the United Kingdom. This type of pedal has a clutch mechanism which must be locked to hold the pedal at any desired point in its travel. The clutch is released by tilting the footplate *forward* and locked by tilting it *backwards* (figures 17 and 18). These actions are carried out by the foot only and between them the pedal is moved by a leg action from the knee. This gives rise to risks less dramatic than capsize, but still quite serious! Should the seat be too close to the drum, it will

34

Figure 17. The forward end of the foot-plate on the 'Premier' pedal is depressed to release the clutch and allow movement of the pedal.

Figure 18. The rear of the foot-plate is depressed by lowering the heel to lock the clutch and hold the desired note. It is important not to sit too close to the drum as it may be difficult to lower the heel far enough to lock the pedal.

sometimes happen that, due to the anatomy of the leg the toe cannot be raised sufficiently to lock the pedal and it must therefore be held by the braced leg muscles while the note is played. This is hard to do, can be rather painful and is distinctly unreliable! If the stool is too far away from the drum and the latter on a polished floor, what happens when the player presses firmly on the pedal is that the drum (even if the brakes are on) slides away from him—possibly even out of reach. The author has personally experienced both of these alarming phenomena when playing in theatre work, where a symphonic type of seat is out of the question due to the need for access to the drum kit, glockenspiel or other 'keyboard' percussion as well as the tympani. Careful experiment must be made to determine a safe working position for the stool and care taken thereafter *not to move it*.

Where only two hand drums are used they will obviously be placed side-by-side with the playing areas adjacent. These will be fitted with a 'drop handle' or 'loose key' screw to provide unobstructed passing from one drum to the other. The 'loose key' is generally the better system as there is no hinge or spring mechanism to rattle and there is never anything projecting inwards over the head as happens in certain positions with a 'drop handle'. When three drums are in use they should be placed approximately on the circumference of a circle in front of the player (figure 19). If four drums are required, however, an arrangement closer to a horseshoe will generally give easier access to the low and high drums.

As already mentioned, alternate beating is the general rule in tympani playing and thus many passages require the playing of a drum by the hand which is *furthest from it*. In other words, for example, a stroke may have to be played on the drum to the player's *right* by his *left* hand, or vice versa. The rule is that the moving hand passes *over* the other hand—which is in any case the easiest and most natural way. This is known as the 'cross-beat' and the action must be practised to get as much of the movement as possible *at the wrist*. The greatest difficulty is that of 'landing' on the new drum *at the proper playing spot* (figure 18). Obviously situations will arise where the cross-beat cannot be used due to the speed of beating required. A cross-beat is a relatively slow stroke and further, if attempted very rapidly the distance which the stick must travel in a short time gives it such velocity that an unintended sforzando usually results. In these circumstances recourse may be had to a 'doubled' beat so as to have the adjacent stick available and thus avoid the cross-beat altogether. In effect a paradiddle is beaten:

R L R R L R L R

Figure 19. The assembly of drums and music stand and the correct position for a standing player. (The author in 1957)

Figure 20. The 'cross beat'. The moving hand passes *over* the other.

The use of this device generally requires to be 'worked out' in advance; it·is hardly possible to do it successfully while sight-reading a part. In any event, it should be used as little as possible.

Where single strokes, reiterated fairly slowly over a long period, are required a smoother and steadier effect is obtained by using the same hand throughout, while if great sonority is wanted, as at the opening of Brahms's First Symphony, two drums may be tuned to the same note and one stick used on each. Great care is needed to ensure that the beats are absolutely simultaneous or the effect is ruined by the resulting 'flams'.

The idiom of the roll is similar to that of the side drum. In general all rolls should start with a firm attack. A firm entry is important even where the roll is a very quiet one, for the tone blends so readily with that of the lower strings, for instance, that the effect of the entry may be entirely lost if it is not accentuated slightly (of course, there are places where the roll should be started without any accent but decisions of this sort are generally best left to the conductor). More commonly one encounters rolls which are not tied over to a final note but come off 'in mid-air'.

This is best executed simply by lifting the sticks off the drum. The tympanist must be able to finish a roll confidently with either hand, otherwise there is apt to be a gap between the penultimate stroke of the roll and the final one. To develop this ability the student should practise rolls timed by a metronome, taking any convenient length, say, two bars 4/4 time with a finishing stroke on the first beat of the next bar, i.e., a roll lasting eight crotchets and finishing with the same hand and with opposite hands, thus:

1. Start left—Finish left
2. Start right—Finish right
3. Start left—Finish right
4. Start right—Finish left.

The metronome, of course, must remain at the same speed for all four. Eventually, the effect should be identical irrespective of which of the four alternatives is used. The metronome speed should be varied from day to day but should *not* be changed within a single practice period. It will be found that the secret lies in speeding up the roll in the last fraction of a second so that whichever hand is required to finish is available. The possession of this ability is unvaluable as it means that the player can have the nearer hand ready to finish a roll which has its final stroke on another drum—a common occurrence. He is also undismayed by rolls on long pauses or final chords and is in no danger of having to finish untidily or risk playing a solo after the rest of the orchestra have 'come off'. Incidentally, this method of practice is very useful for the side drum also, though there the difficulty is not so great.

38

The 'fortepiano' roll requires a special technique for the best results. The initial note should be struck and *allowed to die away* to almost the required dynamic level and the roll then gradually 'insinuated'.

The rate of beating in a roll should be related to the tension of the head and the greatest possible speed is required for the highest notes, especially in loud rolls. A little experiment with the rate near the beginning of a long roll will enable the ear to decide the speed at which the best possible tone is obtained.

Too rapid beating in a head at low tension tends to damp the vibrations and impair the tone. In a crescendo roll rapid beating gives a better and smoother effect especially if the crescendo covers a large dynamic range and occurs over a short time. A moment's reflection will show why. If the beating is rapid the less will be the difference in volume between successive beats so that a smooth curve of 'build up' occurs. Slow beating means a succession of 'steps' and the shorter the crescendo the more audible the 'steps'.

The same grace note embellishments as used on the side drum are occasionally met with in tympani parts. They generally require to be beaten rather more 'openly' than on the side drum to obtain the best effect and, of course, the drag must be beaten L.R.L. or R.L.R. and not 'doubled'.

Where the use of wooden tympani sticks is specified in the part a pair of hard headed xylophone beaters will suffice and no great force should be used or the effect on the head may be disastrous. The use of the reverse end of the normal sticks, which is occasionally required, e.g., Elgar's *Dream of Gerontius* needs no special consideration but pianissimo passages are difficult to control and may be better played with two coins or with the finger-nails (the nail of the middle finger of each hand).

## TUNING AND TONE

It is by their performance in this department of tympani playing that the great are readily distinguished from the not-so-great. Here it is that the player puts his own individual stamp upon his work and that the drummer can (and indeed must) rise to levels of musicianship no lower than those required of any other instrumentalist.

The actual generator of the tone is, of course, the drum head, and too much attention cannot be given to its selection, 'lapping' and mounting on the drum. The best available heads should be purchased (from any reputable manufacturer) and this alone will generally produce a good article which should then be *evenly* 'lapped' by an expert. The drum company will do this if the hoop is sent to them. The next step is the selection of the playing area (i.e. the

**39**

part to be placed next the 'loose key') and this is of great importance as it profoundly influences the results obtained. With today's plastic tympani heads the lapping is machine-done at the factory and the head is purchased already mounted on a metal hoop. The quality is high and the variation from head to head slight if of the same manufacturing model. Within a head there is still some variation from place to place, so that selection of a beating spot may still be desirable but the remainder of what follows is applicable only to calf heads. It is retained for the reasons given earlier, namely that hand drums of copper, with calf heads, are likely to continue in use as 'period' instruments (or 'baroque' tympani).

It is generally possible to see a diametrical marking on the head—a line running right across it and passing through or near the middle. This marks the line of the spine or backbone of the animal from whose skin the head has been made, and the playing spot should *never* be located on it. Most movement in the skin during the animal's life took place *across* the line, not along it, and so the line itself possesses little elasticity. It is in those parts of the head which have greatest elasticity that good tone will be found. The best spot is usually located just to one or other side of the 'backbone line' at one end of it.

The procedure with a new head is therefore to lap it evenly (or have it lapped by an expert) and then mount it on the drum with one end of the 'backbone line' just to the right or left of the loose key (opposite which the playing spot must be). As to which end should go here and which at the other side of the drum the only help that can be given is that generally the white, opaque parts of the head give better tone that the nearly transparent parts—therefore select the end next to which there is most opacity; it can be difficult with some heads. The drum should then be carefully tunes to a good note in the middle of its range and the player should go to a spot at least thirty feet away and *listen* while a friend (preferably a fellow drummer but I have used a horn player with success) taps the head with the stick at the four areas to be examined i.e. one at each side of the 'backbone line' at each end—four in all. It is usually easy to identify the 'right' end because the tone at the 'wrong' end is much poorer. It is less easy to select the better side of the two from the 'right' end as the difference is sometimes very slight and may even be a matter of musical taste. The student should turn his back on the drum and the assistant beating it to ensure that he is uninfluenced by any preconceived ideas. He should hear all areas several times and they should be played to him in different orders so that his decision must be purely a musical one. Finally as a check he can get his friend's opinion while he plays the drum. If the friend has a good ear for tone he will seldom differ in his judgment.

The spot evenutally chosen should be lightly marked with a pencil and the head then mounted with this spot opposite the loose key. *Not only is the best tone obtained in this way but also the best definition of rhythm and pitch.* Of course, it is realized that the complete beginner must usually take his drums as he finds them and this is just as well, for the process described above needs a good ear for tone, which is not acquired overnight. When a player has become discriminating enough to be discontented with the tone of his drums he can rely on being able to mount a new head to the greatest advantage.

### THE TECHNIQUE OF TUNING

The production of determinate musical pitch requires *vibration* at a *single, definite* speed, e.g., 440 vibrations per second is the 'A' of the tuning-fork in New Philharmonic Pitch. In the case of a drum head this means that it must be at the tension necessary for the particular note required and that every part of it must be at that tension. If this latter condition is not fulfilled, the drum, while it *may* give the right note if the tension is correct at and around the playing spot, cannot give its best tone because, in effect, several notes are being sounded simultaneously and probably all within a range of two adjacent semi-tones. Conversely, a drum which is perfectly evenly tensioned will give an equally perfect tone, as long as it is correctly struck. The excellence of the tone is due to the fact that when the whole drum head is generating just one single note, the overtones or harmonics of that note are present in large measure and this greatly improves the musical quality, imparting that bell-like, singing effect which is characteristic of the performance of the finest players. A discussion of the 'harmonic series' of the tympani is outwith the scope of this book, but the student can by a simple experiment establish the truth of this point for himself.

Having tuned a drum carefully and evenly, preferably to a note in the middle of its range, he should bend low over the head just at the playing spot and with as nasal a tone as possible *hum* the note a fifth above that to which the drum is tuned, e.g., if tuned to C, hum G. As the humming is done the drum will 'sing' the hummed note and will do so for some seconds after the humming stops.

The process can be repeated using the note an octave above the note to which the drum is tuned, the third and fifth above that and finally (if his falsetto is good) two octaves above. In actual fact, when the drum is *struck* all these note sound in addition to the 'nominal tone' i.e., the note which predominates and is musically effective in the orchestra. Of course this process operates in all instruments and it is the number and character of the harmonics that govern the tone qualities peculiar to each one, making an oboe sound different from a trumpet and a trumpet from a horn, even when all three sound the same note. The physicist and acoustician tell us that these are not true harmonics and it is certainly the case that a gradual flattening is perceptible as the upper notes are tried. But in ordinary use the lower notes behave sufficiently like harmonics to be regarded as such.

The beginner has now learned the most important thing in the tuning of the tympani, and if he tries the experiment described without success either his drum is not evenly tensioned or he is not humming the notes in tune, or both. The experiment does work, and this raises a vital point—the training of the ear.

Most people aspiring to play the tympani have a reasonable 'musical ear' but this in itself is hardly sufficient for accurate tuning and apart from a few naturally-gifted individuals some training and practice will be required.

The first point is to become thoroughly accustomed to the *sound* of the drums in private practice (i.e., without an orchestra). A useful elementary exercise is to play a note on a piano or other instrument of 'fixed' pitch, tune a drum to it and then, listening carefully, hum the note given out by the drum and compare it with the original piano note. This sort of exercise gets the student accustomed to identifying with accuracy the pitch of the rather nebulous drum tone.

It is much more difficult to hum a note given on a drum than the same note given, say, on a cello. In addition it teaches him to 'hold' a given note while he tunes to it. At first it will be found necessary, after taking the note from the piano or other source, to hum it almost constantly until the drum is correctly in tune but in time he should reach a point where *no humming is necessary at all* and the note is held mentally.

All the tunings given in the 'tutors' should then be practised and care taken to note the changes in *tone* on all the drums as they pass from their lowest to their highest notes, the latter bright, 'punching', quick-speaking and of short reverberation, the former ponderous, 'booming', slow-speaking and long-reverberating. Because of this feature, these low notes must be attacked more firmly than the high notes in an orchestral passage, if a balanced result is to be obtained.

The student should eventually (after a year or two in most cases) be able to tune to within a semitone of any given note merely by recognizing its characteristic tone. The next stage of practice involves changing tuning *without* a piano note, i.e., using the note already on the drum as a reference point and 'pitching' the required note above or below it. This is an essential part of the technique of tuning and involves a knowledge of 'intervals'. As 'interval' in music

42

is simply the distance up or down that one note is from another and every interval has a characteristic sound which the student must get to know. For example, the first two notes of the 'last post' are at an interval of a fifth such as C to G, Bb to F, Eb to Bb, while the first two of 'come to the cook-house door' are at an interval of a major third, such as C to E, Bb to D, Eb to G. Today, not everyone knows these bugle calls and each must find his own example. 'Ba, Ba, black sheep' is a good substitute for the 'last post' as a mnemonic for the interval of a fifth.

Any good book on musical theory deals with the subject in detail and it should present no great obstacle to the student. However, in case of difficulty a music teacher should be able to give lessons on 'ear training' including work on intervals. At first, after making the initial tuning with the help of a piano, the drum should be sounded, its note hummed, then the new note hummed and finally the drum tuned to the new note. Next, only the new note should be hummed and finally the whole process should be done mentally.

Initially, every change should be checked with a piano but later the checks should be less frequent and finally a series of tunings should be attempted and only the initial and final ones checked.

Having indicated the type of study necessary to train the ear some advice on the more practical aspects of tuning the drums may suitably be introduced. First, the method of tuning opposite pairs of handles, so often recommended in the 'tutors', is, I believe, needlessly cumbersome and very much open to the risk of missing a handle. It is certainly wise to become accustomed to turning two handles simultaneously, one with each hand, as the speed gained is of great value in more advanced playing requiring rapid changes of pitch, but each hand should take half the circumference of the drum and work from the playing area forward as illustrated (figures 21 and 22). The head will not be damaged so long as no more than 180° (one half-turn) is given to any handle at a time. That is to say, if more turning than this is required the handles must all be given a half-turn and then *gone over again* giving any extra turning that may be required. Let us suppose that a drum has been tuned as just described and that a tap on the playing spot produces the required note but, as is likely, a poor tone due to variations in tension at other parts of the head. It must be realized that an equal amount of turning applied to every handle *will not produce an even tension in the head although the tuning was known to be perfect before the extra tension was applied.* This is of the utmost importance and must be constantly borne in mind by every tympanist. The explanation is that the elasticity of an animal skin varies from place to place, according to the amount of movement which has occurred during life. The next step in tuning is thus to 'go round' the head and

Figure 21. Alteration of tuning—first pair of handles. Note that *both* sticks are laid down with their shafts *inside* the counter hoop. This removes the risk of knocking the sticks down while leaning over the drum.

Figure 22. Alteration of tuning—second pair of handles. On this particular drum the handle nearest the camera will remain as an 'odd one' to be turned last by the right hand while the left hand prepares to use the 'loose key' at the playing spot.

44

'even up the tuning'. The correct note, we have supposed, is present at the playing spot, which is usual as the drum will have been tried at this spot while the initial tensioning was being done. Starting from there the pitch should be tested at each tuning handle in turn right round the drum, returning to the playing spot. A light stroke should be used at the same distance from the rim all the way round. Generally some points will be found flat and others sharp but it is helpful if in doubt about a particular spot to compare it directly with the pitch at the playing spot, i.e., sounding the doubtful spot and the playing spot in succession several times. It is hardly possible to over-emphasize the importance of *listening* intently—it is the road to ultimate success in every aspect of tympani playing.

The greatest pitfall is that of confusing differences in *tone* with differences in *pitch*. As mentioned earlier no two points on a head give exactly the same tone and it will be found that some parts give a bright 'pinging' quality which tends to sound *sharp*, i.e., too high in pitch, while others give a duller, fuller note which tends to sound *flat*, i.e., too low in pitch. Concentration in listening and mental analysis of the sound heard are the only safeguards. Pitch and quality *can* be heard quite separately with practice and the ability must be cultivated.

In correcting the pitch at flat or sharp points still further traps await the inexperienced. The chief of these arises from failure to appreciate that the turning of a tuning screw influences tension most at the part of the head adjacent to it but produces some difference *everywhere,* even at the other side of the drum. Any reader who is in doubt need only try it, though, of course, he will also find that the nearer he goes to the screw which has been turned, the greater is the effect.

To illustrate the practical importance of this fact an example will serve best. Let us assume, for simplicity's sake, that only one part of the head is out of tune and that it is flat. If the tuning screw at the flat part is given extra turning until the correct pitch is reached the drum will not now—as might be expected—be perfectly tuned, for, while the flat section has been brought up to pitch, the adjoining areas (previously in tune) have been influenced also and made *sharp* requiring further correction. The proper procedure requires anticipation of this effect and much time is saved if it is understood. It is this 'snag' which has before now kept a beginner literally struggling for hours to get a proper tuning; as one defect is corrected another appears. General rules cannot be laid down for this problem as every head has its own peculiarities and they must be discovered before tuning will become reliable. The best heads, of course, have least variation but none are entirely uniform. Some parts may tension rapidly while others may require much more turning of the screw for a given rise in pitch. The best method of 'getting to know the head' is to tune evenly to a note low in the range of the drum and then give each handle *exactly* the same amount of turning, say a half-turn, and note the effect on pitch at all points round the head. The tuning should then be 'evened up' and the process repeated till the top of the range is reached. In this way the student will soon learn which screws will need more and which less than the average amount of turning for a given change of pitch. In all but 'emergency' changes of pitch the 'loose key' or 'drop handle' *must* be used exactly as the other tuning screws. I have heard other views on this but common sense indicates what experiment proves—that there is no reason to treat the 'loose key' differently from the other screws where tuning is concerned. So far, only tuning 'up', i.e., increasing the tension has been considered and in tuning 'down' the same general principles apply but there is an important practical point to be noted. After the screws have been turned the palm of the hand should be placed on the centre of the head and gentle but firm pressure made *downwards* on it. If this is not done the head will not relax to the extent allowed by the loosening of the screws due to its tendency to 'bind' or simply to stick to the edge of the shell. The usual result is that to get the desired pitch the screws are loosened further than really necessary and as soon as the head is struck hard at the next entry a dismal downward glissando occurs as the 'binding' is undone. This particular piece of technique, for reasons to be given later, is not relevant to pedal tympani.

Having covered most of the 'groundwork' of tuning let us now turn to the problem of keeping in tune during an orchestral performance—not so straightforward a task as it might be thought. There are two main difficulties and the first of these is atmospheric variation. The atmosphere varies in several ways, the most obvious of which is in temperature, but the most important of which is in *humidity*—the amount of water vapour in the atmosphere. All natural drum heads are very susceptible to a moist atmosphere and lose tension. With the tympani the effect is worse for not only is there loss of tone but, of course, the loss of tension causes the drum to go flat. On a wet night, even a few minutes after tuning, the notes may be distinctly flat while the highest notes in the drums' range may be unobtainable. The only remedy for this latter trouble is to obtain the note on a smaller drum, where it will lie in the middle or lower part of the range. In general, in wet weather, the tuning must be constantly watched and before playing a work the final tuning delayed till the last possible moment.

Even in dry weather, the humidity of the air in a hall tendes to increase during the evening as the air breathed out by the audience is laden with moisture. If a previously moist atmosphere should start

46

to dry, as may happen for instance if frost sets in, the drums will 'dry out' and become sharp. To cut a long story short, it is *never* safe to go on the playform, tune the drums, depart for half-an-hour for refreshment or other purposes and return to play without checking the tuning. Equally, one must guard against 'day-dreaming', say, in oratorios where not merely bars of rest but items of rest are usual, and remember to watch the pitch in preparation for the next entry. The other difficulty is that of adjusting the *tuning* according to the *volume to be produced*. It is insufficiently realized even in some high circles, that a given tension *will not produce the same note* over the whole dynamic range. *The greater the volume, the flatter is the pitch produced immediately after the stroke.* The effect is most marked in wet weather and in experiments controlled carefully by reliable observers and checked by recording I have found that a note played as a heavy fortissimo may be as much as a semi-tone flat by comparison with the note resulting from a quiet pianissimo stroke. In other words, a player unaware of this effect could tune his instruments perfectly with the usual quiet taps and then, if his first entry happened to be a loud one, find himself so flat as even to be in a different key. It is true, of course, that no matter how hard or how lightly the drum is struck, the final aftertone as it dies away is at the same pitch—but the final aftertone is not heard in a loud tutti and what *is* heard is the *pitch produced immediately after the stroke*. The pitch is flattest at that point and gradually rises as the note dies away. The explanation of the phenomenon is, I believe, simple.

The head is an elastic membrane and the note produced depends not only on the tension but also on the *length* of it. A heavy blow stretches the head sufficiently to make it significantly longer for a fraction of a second, and a lower note is produced. As the note dies away the head 'springs back' to its original length and gives a slightly higher pitch. What, then, is the practical application of all this? It is clearly impossible to be constantly adjusting the tension and the player should select a mean value to suit the bulk of the work to be played. For example in a Haydn Symphony most of the playing will be in loud tuttis, whereas a modern work might contain little but piano rolls. The essential point is that the player *must be prepared to adjust for passages of special importance.* If having played through almost the whole of a work without exceeding a mezzopiano, he finds a solo roll fortissimo in the last four bars, the tuning must be sharpened or it will sound flat. Conversely, if in the course of a work which is mostly forte and louder he is confronted by a solo passage pianissimo the tuning must be flattened or the solo will sound sharp. As the stretching affects mainly the area around the 'playing spot' it is generally sufficient to adjust only the screws acting on that part of the head. Naturally there are occasions where there is not time for adjustment and the tympanist must consider whether he should sacrifice accuracy during a tutti to get a solo in tune. Generally speaking I think it is worth it. As in so many matters the ultimate problem is not 'how' but 'how much' and in this only experience, a reliable ear and an artistic sense can help. But even the beginner is much better off if he understands the nature of the difficulty and learns much more quickly to meet it effectively.

There remains to be considered that part of the tympanist's skill which gives him an aura of mystery evoking the awe of the layman and compelling the respect even of horn-players—his ability to change tuning while the orchestra is playing.

There is not, as is popularly supposed, a single 'magic password' to success in this difficult attainment. As in others, mastery is compounded of a number of contributory skills, some of which are quite 'down to earth' and not at all mystic. Certainly, they are not outwith the scope of any musical person and require no special gift such as 'absolute pitch'. What they *do* need is a great deal of practice.

There are broadly two methods by which information about the pitch of a drum can be obtained while the orchestra is playing, the first mechanical, the second musical. The mechanical method includes two factors, the tuning mechanism and the head itself. With experience, the player can have quite an accurate idea of the pitch of a drum from the ease or difficulty of turning the tuning screws, but more important he gets to know the approximate amount of alteration in pitch produced by different amounts of turning and in time can even allow fairly accurately for variations in atmospheric conditions. In practising tuning, part of the study should always be given to this purely mechanical aspect, with, as already indicated, special attention to determine any parts of the head requiring more or less than average turning of the screws. Some players, by feeling the tension of the head with the finger-tips, can associate it with the pitch of the drum. Personally, I can do this only very roughly and have not devoted any practice specifically to developing the ability as I believe that other methods are more reliable and no more difficult. But some people may be naturally gifted and every player should test his own ability in this direction.

The second, musical method, likewise involves two factors. Firstly, the pitch of the drum may be compared with some readily identifiable note in the music being played by the orchestra—a holding note on the horn is ideal. This may be used to check the existing pitch of a drum or more often to check the pitch *after a change in tuning has been made.* In this connection a knowledge of the score is a great help to the tympanist, who, when faced with a change of pitch during a work, can very often find an instrument playing the note required during the rest preceding the entry of the new note. As suggested, a holding note on a prominent instrument is ideal, but obviously not always obtainable and the required note from any source (so long, of course, as the tympanist can *hear* the instrument playing it) sounding for even a second or two is sufficient for an experienced player. In such a case, then, an approximate tuning would be made 'mechanically' as soon as the last passage on the 'old' tuning was completed and then adjusted musically to be accurate by comparison with the 'reference note' in the orchestra. A change of tuning on the drums is usually required because the music is about to modulate to a different key and frequently the new key is established before the tympani enter. In that event, especially where the drums are to be tuned to the tonic and dominant of the new key, reference notes are unnecessary as the relation of the notes to the new tonality will be obvious when it appears. In very chromatic music of the 'modern' type, however, these convenient aids may be little if at all available and the player must rely on the second line of approach in which he uses the notes on the drums themselves as 'reference notes'. This is more difficult. The drum note is not at all easy to hear in an orchestral tutti, particularly if it is a note foreign to the key in use at the particular moment and to 'hear mentally' the required new note derived by interval is even more difficult, especially as the player is likely to be watching the conductor and counting bars at the same time. But there is a practice technique which can be helpful. It is to practice with a radio or record player playing and listening to the note of a tuning fork (or better still a drum, if it can be arranged) 'fixing' the note mentally and 'hearing' various intervals from it, tuning the drum if available and subsequently checking the results with the music 'turned off'. The most difficult form of all is where a change is required on all the drums and one is eventually left without any 'proved' note until the next entry. In all tuning which must be done without a 'reference note' in the orchestra the tympanist has in some degree to isolate himself mentally from the orchestra while still, so to speak, 'keeping a window open' through which he can watch the conductor, count the rests and so on. There is no denying that this is difficult and takes some time to acquire; it probably never become a hundred per cent efficient, but I have not heard of any drummers developing 'split personality' in the attempt!

Sometimes an alteration in tuning has to be carried out in such a short space of time that the proper procedure cannot possibly be used. This is especially the case in modern works where the composer may have had in mind the use of 'machine drums' with instantaneous tuning. All that can be done is to change the tension at and around the playing spot by turning the two nearest handles and the two next to these, if there is enough time. It is usually impossible to check the result before playing and such changes must be practised in advance to discover how much turning is required and how many handles can be reached in the available time. The resulting tone can never be very good as in fact the head will be sounding two or more notes simultaneously. The most noticeable effect is usually a *pulse* or beat in the tone, such as occurs when two instruments supposedly playing in unison are not exactly in tune with each other.

Incidentally, the absence of such a beat, or 'heterodyne effect' as the acousticians term it, is quite a useful way of deciding whether the tuning of a drum is accurate enough if there is not time to 'go round' the head. A firm beat should be made and the tone listened to carefully; if a pulse is only just audible or better still absent entirely, the tuning is accurate enough for all practical purposes.

With regard to trying the pitch of the drums while the orchestra is playing, there is much argument about whether it should be done with the stick or by the finger. The method of using the finger is to press the tip of the middle finger, slightly moistened, *gently* down on the head at the playing spot and then to force it smartly forwards and upwards. Nevertheless the stick probably gives a more true indication of the pitch, as the finger technique gives a high proportion of the upper harmonics, which may be confusing. With either method, the important this is to do the testing during relatively loud tuttis only; it can be quite audible during, say, a quiet string passage.

Calf drum heads do not last for ever and in time gradually lose their tone quality much as a violin string does, but with proper care they will last many seasons, especially in amateur use, where they may be played only once or twice a week.

A muted or muffled effect is occasionally required (coperti). This is usually obtained by placing a damping pad at the side of the drum, immediately inside the hoop. This reduces the ring of the note, but also obscures the pitch. A better result is given by a pad placed at the *centre* of the head, which reduces the ring but does not obscure the pitch.

### TUNING WITH PEDAL TYMPANI

The problems of tuning, considered above at some length, are greatly simplified by the combination of plastic heads, pedal tuning and tuning gauges (invariably fitted to pedal tympani). The plastic head is virtually unaffected by humidity and little affected by changes in temperature; movement of the pedal applies tension uniformly throughout the circumference of the head, and the gauge allows that a note will be, if not precisely correct, very nearly so. The advantages of the plastic head are thus self-evident and nothing more need be said about them, but there are some disadvantages. While a very precise pitch is produced, it is a 'thin' sound lacking the richness and fullness of a good calf head. But it is nearly impossible to use calf heads on modern pedal tympani and this must simply be accepted. The older models of pedal drum were, of course, used with calf heads, as the plastic variety did not exist but today, even in these instruments, it is rare to find calf heads. The ease of identifying the pitch of the drums with plastic heads is popular not only with tympanists but also with conductors and audiences. It remains true, however, that some of the most perceptive individuals complain of the loss of tone quality. There is another element in this. Because of their limited elasticity, compared with calf heads, the tone quality on the lower notes of the range of any given drum is so poor that these notes must be avoided (with perhaps occasional exception for a quiet passage) and only the middle and upper part of the range used. The low notes must be obtained as middle range notes on the *next larger* size of drum. This has led ultimately to the manufacture of a drum of 32 inch diameter—larger than was ever required for calf heads—to obtain the occasional notes below the low F. But, of course, these notes lie in the middle range of so large a drum, and the whole system, from the smallest to the largest drums, has deprived us of the characteristic sound of the low notes of the tympani—and hence of the intentions of composers who wrote with that specific effect in mind. With this practice there has developed a tendency to play everything on 'oversize' drums, i.e. one size larger than would normally have been standard practice. The result is that some of the higher notes are deficient in tone and resonance, though not in pitch, because the diameter of the drum is technically too large for such notes. The plastic head is much more resistant to insult than the calf head, and much less expensive, but they do nonetheless gradually lose tone with continued use and should of course be replaced at the first sign of deterioration. In an instrument in which tone quality, along with intonation, is so large a measure of musical success, and cultivation of the player's ear so crucial, it is ridiculous to persevere with equipment which has passed its best and will no longer give a fine result even in the most skilled hands.

It is appropriate at this stage to include some factors relevant to tone productions not considered previously among the basic essentials of the subject. A single note on the tympani may be conceived as three separate phases (though, of course, one continuous sound). The first is the 'impact phase' consisting largely of the surface noise of the attack and hence obscuring the essential tone quality of the drum. It is of very short duration and gives way to the 'bell phase', the characteristic fine ringing quality and well defined pitch of a properly tuned drum. This is of much longer duration that the 'impact phase', its apparent duration in the orchestra depending on the orchestral texture and dynamic at the time. During the 'bell phase' the pitch rises gradually, as explained previously, and continues to do so as that phase merges into the third phase—the final aftertone, which will not normally be heard in the ensemble unless the drum happens to be solo. Two very practical points follow from this. First, a tympani note should never be so quickly damped that the 'bell phase' has not emerged, resulting in something which is almost all 'impact phase' and sounds little better than a gunshot—unless, of course, that is the composer's intention! Secondly, and of even greater importance is that the speed of rolls should be kept to the *minimum* necessary to keep the head in vibration and produce a continuous sound. The more rapid the beating, beyond this point, the greater becomes the proportion of the sound contributed by the 'impact phase' at each stroke and the less the proportion of 'bell phase' with resulting loss of tone. Each successive stroke falls before the 'bell phase' is fully developed. A roll is thus in danger of becoming a continuous 'impact phase'. The pitch of the roll note, as explained earlier, will also be flatter than that of single notes from the same drum and, depending on the musical content, allowance may have to be made for this.

Tuning with the pedal will be found relatively easy by those with experience of hand drums. Notes *should always be approached from below*, which is why the hand drum technique of pressing on the head when lowering the pitch is irrelevant. There is an important point to note. In instruction manuals or 'tutors' the student is told to relax the pedal to its lowest point, hum the note required and press the pedal, locking it when the appropriate pitch is reached. This will give the note only if sounded by sympathetic vibration, i.e. by humming into the drum or playing the same note on another drum. The lightest stroke with a stick will yield a flatter pitch. This is because a drum tuned in that way to a particular note is being tuned *to its aftertone*—the sharpest possible pitch obtainable from that tension of the head and so quiet as to have no practical use unless for sympathetic vibration to reinforce the tone of another drum playing the same note—a very occasional requirement. Thus, having tuned in that way the pitch must be sharpened (as explained earlier, for hand drums) to a degree commensurate with the dynamic required. Pedal tuning is more or less instantaneous—provided it is 'correct first time', but the foot is not so precise an instrument as the hand and if the movement has to be repeated, the whole process is often no quicker than making a change on hand drums. Careful damping is essential to prevent audible glissandi. Some instruments are fitted with a fine adjustment mechanism which may be hand or foot operated, the latter being the better as it can be used while both hands are occupied in playing an orchestral part. As described earlier, the foot and leg actions are very different with the clutch mechanism of Premier drums and the 'balanced action' of Ludwig drums. It is simply a matter of familiarity and the acquisition of facility. There exists a third type of pedal action—the Dresden pedal. This involves a heel-operated clutch and is rare in the United Kingdom. Any reader happening to meet this instrument should seek guidance in the specialist texts noted in the bibliography.

Tuning gauges have taken much of the worry out of re-tuning during a work, especially where dissonant notes have to be found, i.e. notes foreign to the tonality prevailing while the change is being made. Using the gauge, the player can be sure of being at least very near to his note which can be finally adjusted by ear. It cannot be over-stressed that tuning must remain an exercise *for the ear* and that the gauge is only an aid, being quite approximate. It is also an aid which must be checked and adjusted *by ear* every time it is used. A device with so many mechanical moving parts slips easily out of adjustment.

The common availability of pedal drums has resulted in a much more free style of writing in tympani parts, the player often being left to make his own tuning indications. In this regard, some very helpful advice is given by James Holland in his book 'Percussion' in the series of Yehudi Menuhin Music Guides.

Compositions for solo pedal tympani have appeared. Their musical merit may be subject for discussion and argument, there being those who believe that the drum is a better instrument in accompaniment than as soloist! At all events, those who aspire to enter the colleges and academies of music with a view to a professional qualification and subsequent career will find themselves obliged to play at least some of it.

There is often discussion about the best second instrument for a percussionist and the piano is recommended by many because of its obvious relevance to the glockenspiel, xylophone, marimba and vibraphone. Although 'sent to the piano' in childhood myself, this is not a view which I endorse personally; most musicians are familiar with the layout of a piano keyboard and only that minimal knowledge is of value in the elementary study of keyboard percussion. Of much more value to the tympanist is the study of an instrument in which the intonation is in the hands of the player, not the piano tuner. The best choice is probably an instrument of approximately the same pitch as the tympani, such as the 'cello, the horn or the trombone. With the latter, the student soon becomes aware that F sharp and G flat are not the same note. The difference is an easily measurable distance on a trombone slide. On the horn, the player makes this adjustment with his hand in the bell of the instrument, the 'cellist on the finger-board. These instruments develop an acute awareness of pitch and an ability to cope with fractions of a semitone such as are the common requirement of a tympanist. No amount of piano playing, fixed as it is to equal temperament, develops this ability. An ear for fine tone is also developed only on an instrument on which the player has to *make* the sound and this is just as vital as an acute ear for pitch, and an even rarer ability than precise perception of pitch. The ear, especially in regard to tone, is the ultimate limiting factor in striving for success as a tympanist. Once a player no longer hears a difference between his own results and those of the finest players, he has reached his ceiling, which is probably a biologically predetermined level in each individual. Natural endowment (which is essential) can be developed, often remarkably, by good teaching and hard work by the student who must, throughout his playing life, never lose the habit of listening critically to the work of every tympanist he hears—and most especially his own.

Really good heads, without eccentricities of any kind, such as a tendency to emphasize some of the very high and dissonant harmonics, are scarce and worth looking after carefully. The drums should be fitted with robust wooden covers which should always be put on when the instruments are not in use. A drum which is constantly troublesome in tuning and unwilling to give a 'true' note should be carefully examined to ensure that it is *perfectly circular* before scrapping what may be a good head. It is a waste of money to put new heads on misshapen drums.

With regard to performing there is not a great deal of advice that can be given. The main thing is to acquire confidence and to play just what is written. Notes must often be damped to prevent their ringing on beyond the written value. This is done by drawing the tips of the middle, ring and little fingers *lightly* over the head, the stick being held by finger and thumb. For repeated notes it is scarcely possible to do it effectively if the speed of the beats exceeds about 120 per minute. The drum must always be damped after the final stroke of a roll concluding a work or movement.

If the part calls for a fortissimo roll, a mezzopiano one ruins the effect. A tentative performance on any instrument is bad but on the tympani it is worse for the reason that, feeling a lack of support, the whole orchestra becomes tentative and indecisive. A reliable tympanist is an enormous asset to any conductor, for he alone can 'pull up' a tutti that is gaining in speed despite every effort from the rostrum and in other instances he can virtaully produce order out of chaos with a confident entry that every player can recognize and so 'get his bearings'. So far as the tympanist is concerned, the better the orchestra, the easier it is to play in. A second-rate orchestra makes the job difficult because several versions of a note may be current simultaneously and the player, in tuning, must select one without any certainty that it will be the popular version of that note by the time his entry is reached. In professional circles, it is largely the absence of these irregularities of intonation that distinguishes the great orchestras from the less great.

Perhaps most important of all is the cultivation of a dynamic sense; the lack of it is responsible for a great deal of very unmusical playing. Forte in a Mozart overture is not the same as forte in a Sibelius symphony or Wagner overture, and I cannot do better than conclude by recommending my readers with all possible emphasis to cultivate *discretion* in their playing and so place beyond doubt their claim to a musical status equal to that of any other instrumentalist.

# 3. THE XYLOPHONE AND GLOCKENSPIEL, MARIMBA AND VIBRAPHONE

IN A BOOK of this size it is impossible to deal exhaustively with all the instruments on which a percussionist may be required to perform, but I have chosen to include some advice on these closely-related instruments in the belief that the competent side drummer will have little difficulty in 'picking up' the technique of such things as the tambourine and castanets, cymbals and triangle if he watches carefully the methods of good players at as close a range as possible.

Once again, nothing is included here that can be found elsewhere, e.g., in 'tutors' or textbooks of orchestration.

The best thing that can be done is to purchase a 'tutor'—several good ones are readily avialable—and to work steadily at the recommended exercises. As soon as reasonable fluency is attained the student should learn a few solos by *heart*, and take every opportunity to perform them in public. He can either purchase solos specially written or arranged for the instrument or adapt works of his own choice suitable for the idiom of the instrument. There is a wide choice and even some of the works of Bach, Handel and Mozart are not unacceptable if tastefully played with a good piano or orchestral accompaniment. Violin solos of the more florid type are a good source of 'raw material'.

The value of this type of playing is that it imparts *confidence* (very necessary to a drummer unaccustomed to playing the 'tune') and a facile technique (allowing him to concentrate mainly on the music and conductor when playing in the orchestra).

### SIGHT READING

The main difficulty of the instruments for orchestral purposes is that of *sight-reading*, because, unlike other melody instruments, the *sense of touch* cannot be used on them. The player must therefore *watch* the instrument and beaters to some extent and much practice should be done from music (as opposed to playing from memory) to cultivate the ability to play with only an occasional glance at the instrument. The eye is capable of seeing *in detail* only the spot that is actually being watched, e.g., the music, but it perceives in a more hazy way the surroundings as well—and the instrument is part of those surroundings. To prove this to himself the reader need only look fixedly at a word in the top line of any page in this book. He cannot read the words in the bottom line of the page, but he can appreciate that there is printing there and half-way up the page he may be able to see that there are separate words, though he cannot read them without taking his eye off the top line.

The detail is greater with objects very close to the one actually being 'fixed' by the eye. The xylophone player must learn to work as much as possible on this ring of hazy, 'outer' vision—peripheral vision as it is technically known. Naturally, in performing, the music should be as close to the instrument as possible (consistent with being so placed as to make it easy to glance at the conductor) and ideally both the instrument *and* the conductor should be within the visual field—the conductor visible dimly above the music or just to one side of it, the instrument just below the music. Of course this is not always possible and it is as well to practise sometimes with the music raised fairly high above the instrument to allow some margin for occasions when it cannot be set only just above the instrument, or when the eyes must deviate a lot to see the conductor, as is often the case when playing in a theatre 'pit'.

When all this has been said, however, it must be freely admitted that fluency in sight-reading is more difficult to achieve on the xylophone than on any other instrument and a high standard will be reached only by the few players who make it their principal study.

The majority (including soloists who must perform from memory) have to be content to remain moderate sight-readers. Fortunately, composers and arrangers know this, and xylophone parts usually include fairly frequent rests in which the player can read the next few bars and then keep the instrument in view while playing them. This ability to 'photograph' mentally a few bars at a time is very useful and should also be practised. At first the part must be watched most of the time but gradually more can be 'taken in' at a glance. Difficult passages, too, are not usually too long to be easily memorized and experience of solo playing is of great assistance. To sum up then, the xylophone player performs his solos from memory but in the orchestra reads his part by a combination of true reading and memory work, the proportion varying from player to player. Those who find memorizing difficult will largely read the part, from necessity, while those who memorize easily will rely chiefly on that. The well-known finding with players of other instruments that the best sight-readers can play little from memory and that those who play well from memory and 'by ear' are usually poor sight-readers, is even more conspicuous among xylophone players. Memorizing itself needs some practice for although individuals vary greatly in natural ability the least gifted can improve him or herself. Some succeed better with a visual memory of the music; others prefer not to think of the printed copy but just of 'the tune' and the pattern of movement of the hammers.

Since the first edition of this book in 1957, demands upon the orchestral player of these instruments (the 'keyboard percussion') have greatly increased, with long and difficult passages, much harder to memorize and thus virtually requiring fluent sight-reading. There has thus tended to emerge a specialist player, generally an individual who has unusual natural ability with his or her peripheral vision, ideally associated with a particular pleasure in playing this group of instruments. It should be remembered that, in sight-reading with peripheral vision, a part of the central nervous system is being required to perform a function for which it is not naturally equipped. It therefore exhausts quickly, especially in the early stages of practice, when sessions should be short, 'a little and often' being the principle to adopt. Natural endowment varies greatly and only the really gifted are likely to become highly competent. None of the foregoing, of course, affects solo playing which must be done from memory.

### TECHNIQUE

The beaters should be held lightly in almost the same way as the right-hand drum stick, the difference being that the stick is held at the *last* joint of the index finger and that the middle finger also takes part in the grip.

The roll is a succession of single strokes, evenly beaten, and tone production is easier than with the tympani but depends on just the same general principles. The wrist action is different, however, as the palms of the hand are directed almost straight downwards, and it is, I think, better not to practise the xylophone, if possible, while much tympani playing is being done or vice versa. This ensures the highest possible standard on either instrument but is obviously impossible where a single player is required to play all instruments, e.g., in theatre work. The side drum, however, goes well with either and may be freely practised and played.

Much effective solo playing can be done with three and four hammers and the grip is illustrated to make the technique quite clear (figures 23 and 24).

As in tympani playing, alternate beating is the rule but often such devices as the side drum 'daddy-mummy' (for 'paired' notes in quick passages) and the paradiddle are valuable and may greatly simplify some otherwise awkward passages, e.g.,

58

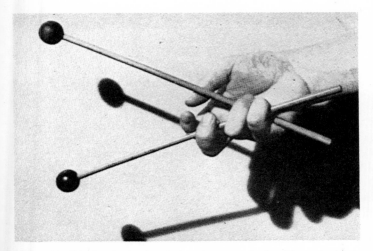

Figure 23. Grip for the beaters in four-hammer playing. The outer beater (lower one in the photograph) is held by the index and middle fingers. The inner beater is held by the thumb and third finger pressing against the stick in opposite directions.

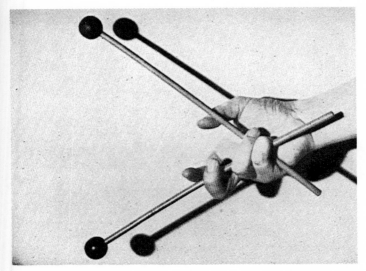

Figure 24. Method of obtaining a larger interval. The distance is increased by pressing outwards (i.e. in opposite directions) with thumb and index finger. A squeezing action by the third finger reduces the distance.

Except in very rapid scale passages, where accidentals may be struck on the end of the bar, it should be the rule to strike in the centre of the bars, as this gives the best tone.

Two types of beaters at least are required, one with hard heads and another with a slightly softened head, e.g., hard rubber which is only just *slightly* compressible. Soft rubber beaters may be used to minimize noise in practice but as much as possible should be done with the normal beaters as the balance is very different with soft rubber heads.

For the marimba and vibraphone soft mallets are normally used, 'graded' after the fashion of tympani sticks. It is important that hard beaters are *not* used on the marimba as the bars (which are thinner than those of the xylophone) may be damaged. With their greater sustaining power both the marimba and vibraphone are specially adapted to chord playing with four hammers. The vibraphone is the more versatile of the two instruments and has established for itself a prominent position as a solo instrument in the field of jazz. Here the player must acquire a knowledge of chords and keyboard harmony almost to the level of a pianist and can enjoy exercising his individuality and inventiveness in a way which only jazz allows.

The xylophone is a very agile instrument but one hundred per cent accuracy is hard to achieve, for the player is often attempting with the relatively cumbersome mechanism of wrists and hammers, passages which would not come without difficulty to instrumentalists who have the much more nimble equipment of their fingers acting upon keys. Fortunately, however, the short 'chippy' quality of the xylophone tends to minimize rather than to exaggerate the occasional wrong note which is to be heard even in the highest professional circles.

It will by now be evident that 'the complete percussion player' has to be a man or woman of some versatility and capable of hard work but it is this very variety in the work which is so attractive.

In the orchestra, the percussion player is very much a soloist, needing the courage of his convictions and a sense of responsibility and independence. It is a discipline that develops qualities of character of great value far from any orchestra or band and it remains for me only to hope that my readers have found this book helpful and that as percussion players they will have as much pleasure and satisfaction as I have had and hope to continue having.

60

# 4. SOME MEDICAL ASPECTS OF PERCUSSION PLAYING

ANY ATTEMPT at a complete treatise on the medical aspects of percussion playing would call for a separate volume several times the size of this one. Nevertheless, the increasing importance of the topic to the majority of players, with wider coverage in this edition to include material relevant to the more experienced and senior performer. make the inclusion of this brief section mandatory. The absence of any but the shortest reference to medical aspects in the first edition merely reflected the fact that percussionists at that time gave it little attention and that the text was aimed at the younger and less experienced player, with whom the medical aspects scarcely arose.

An important point of anatomy, however, was included—namely that 'the muscles of the wrist' (often referred to in tutors) do not really exist. The power for drumming comes from muscles in the forearm and to a lesser extent in the hand; the fingers are also moved by forearm muscles. The wrist is simply a hinge at which most of the movement occurs. This is why, when practising, discomfort is felt in the forearm. If the forearm is stretched out, parallel with the floor, palm of the hand facing downwards, the very powerful muscle group on the under (i.e. the palm) side of the forearm are the *flexors* of the wrist and mainly deliver the strokes of percussion playing. On the opposite (upper) side are the *extensors* of the wrist, a less powerful group, mainly responsible for the recovery action, i.e. the upward 'flick' which should follow every stroke and upon which, therefore, tone quality largely depends. Readers will recognise that the position described is more or less that used for the right-hand side drumstick (both sticks in the 'matched' grip) or for the xylophone, etc. It is not the position recommended for general tympani playing, though it has useful applications there, as described earlier. In the recommended position the forearm is partly rotated, which results in muscle groups working in combination to give a greater force. The point is further demonstrated in the illustrations. At one time there used to occur a condition known as 'drummers' palsy' (or paralysis). This was damage to, or even rupture of, the long extensor tendon of the thumb. It would happen

61

Figure 25. The author (right) in conversation with Dr Geoffrey Walsh during an electromyographic study of stick action in the laboratories of the Department of Physiology, University of Edinburgh.

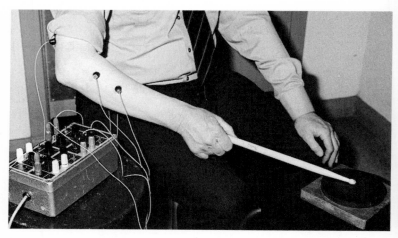

Figure 26. The apparatus for obtaining the input to the electromyograph. Suction cup silver chloride electrodes are applied to the skin overlying the muscle being studied. The side drum stick is used on a normal practice pad.

in the left hand and only with the type of grip used by English, German and American players. The Scottish and Austrian grip *flexes* the thumb and so could never overtax an extensor tendon. In any event it must now be very rare. I have never seen a case, or even heard of one. The injury would result from overworking the tendon. Perhaps drummers, even in military service, where I believe the condition would have been mainly seen, are not as hard working as they were in the past. Today's marching bands do a good deal of their marching in trucks! A blister at the base of the right index finger after a long march is, even today, by no means rare in a player unaccustomed to heavy playing for so long a spell.

The physiology, relating to the *action* of muscles, is no less important than an understanding of their anatomy—their positions and connections. To produce its action a muscle contracts, so pulling on the tendon connected to hand or fingers, and then relaxes, allowing a return to the original position. This is the sequence in a single stroke of percussion playing such as might form part of a single stroke roll—a roll, say, on tympani or xylophone. It is essential to appreciate that there is a definite limit to the frequency at which this action can be repeated. This is normally about seven times per second when only the hand or finger itself has to be moved. A trill on a wood-wind instrument would be a good example. The percussion player has to move a beater of some sort and could expect to do a little less. The writer, in the experiments illustrated, comfortably achieved just under seven strokes per second. Any attempt to play faster than seven beats per second will quickly lead to spasm and slowing. The Latin-American percussionist, using his fingers only, on bongoes, can achieve a faster roll very briefly (which he may call a 'nerve roll') and very exciting it sounds— but it must be stopped before spasm sets in, resulting in a dismal

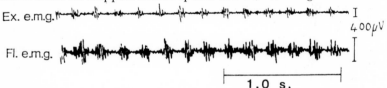

Figure 27. Electromyogram of the forearm flexor and extensor muscles during a single roll (right hand only) of moderate force and speed (approximately 6 beats per second). The upper trace shows the extensor activity, with an upward 'flick' for each beat. The lower trace shows the individual beats themselves, the bar at the bottom representing one second of time.

anti-climax as the roll slows down! Mention of spasm brings us naturally to a consideration of the opposite of spasm—relaxation. It is an absolute necessity for good technique on any instrument. Most people think they know what it means for it is much talked and written about in relation to almost every kind of human activity. Yet a satisfactory scientific definition does not exist! Perhaps the best advice is to experience it in this way. Lift gently the paw of a sleeping cat or dog, or the forearm of a young child, and let it drop. The sensation imparted is that of complete relaxation. In instrumental performance relaxation implies the ability to carry out whatever technical manoeuvres may be required by the music without any sensation of stiffness or resistance in the muscles, the movements flowing in an almost liquid way, irrespective of whether they involve a heavy fortissimo or the lightest pianissimo. This requires a high degree of training in the muscles, a perfectly clear mental grasp of the figurations and the total confidence in one's ability engendered by these. This leads to a scrutiny of the psychological aspects of performing, probably the largest and certainly the most difficult area. In anatomy and physiology we have to deal with clearly demonstrable fact. In psychology we have to work among the myriad subtleties of human individuality and behaviour. What is sure and reliable one day, in a given set of circumstances, may be quite unsure with the same individual on another occasion. We are on shifting sands. And there is an intimate and individual interplay between the psychological and the physiological in terms of muscle action and relaxation, or the lack of it.

Taking the obvious first, percussion playing is not for the naturally timid or self-effacing. This is not to imply arrogance or brashness, but to underline the ability to accept musical responsibility and to remain reasonably calm and effective when under the considerable stress which does arise occasionally in most types of playing. One does not seek the stolid individual who experiences no excitement: he will give a dull performance.

The prime requirement for relaxation is confidence. This is why the young player generally, though not invariably, seems to have it naturally. His skills are recently acquired, like his ability to swim, ride his bicycle, sail a boat, etc. He *knows* he will not sink, or fall off the bicycle and in the same way he knows for a certainty that he can produce a smooth side drum roll or whatever else may be required of him. He rejoices in his abilities and probably practises more than necessary. With all this comes perfect relaxation and a good technique. As a player matures, advances into and through adult life, the situation changes. He may no longer have adequate practice time or the time for proper exercise such as swimming or cycling. He may have to spend too much of his day indoors and all of this leads to a general decline in physical fitness, which plays no small part in relaxation and successful performance. He also acquires insight into his musical activities with greater awareness of the serious effects of any lapse and hence the beginnings of apprehension about his ability always to play the part perfectly. This is the earliest phase of 'performing nerves'. It is, of course, a reaction not peculiar to orchestral playing or indeed to musicians, but is common in all walks of life subject to much stress. So common is it that some of our stock phrases are derived from it; we speak of being 'scared stiff' or 'shaking with fright', for some people become tense while others develop a tremor. Despite the frequency of the condition we have no idea why this division exists or what the mechanisms are, but it is common knowledge that an individual may easily be reduced to complete uselessness by it. 'Stage fright' is a typical example in which the mental impairment may be so severe that he or she cannot utter a word.

What can be done about it? Relief is often sought in drugs but a *remedy* requires a return to a healthier life-style. A good diet, adequate rest and sleep, sufficient exercise and fresh air, and, of course, sufficient time for practice are the essentials. Given these, confidence will return and with it the necessary relaxation. The percussionist is perhaps more at risk from loss of relaxation than many other instrumentalists. A key is either open or closed, a valve is up or down; there are no intermediate requirements. From single stroke to double stroke and through 'multiple bounce' rolls (as open crush rolls are sometimes termed) to closed crush rolls represents a finely graded sequence of controlled muscle tension in the hands and forearms not unlike the muscular adjustments of embouchure of the wind player. Complete relaxation may occasionally elude even those who normally have little trouble. When this happens one sometimes sees drummers doing strange twisting exercises with a pair of sticks. These exercises, which are essentially static, are of little use because drumming is a matter of movement. The best remedy is to take a pair of tympani sticks (or side drum sticks held by the 'wrong' end) and to roll on a cushion at moderate speed and with moderate force until the weaker hand begins to falter. After a rest of ten to fifteen minutes it will be found that complete relaxation has been achieved. If a player is seriously out of practice a longer period of rest will be needed.

Drugs are mentioned above in the context of relief from the symptoms of 'nerves' in the concert hall. Individuals vary so greatly that it would be foolish to offer specific advice but some general points apply universally. The effect of a drug at a given time depends on the dosage and the time of administration. Both of these can be very difficult to determine—and a misjudgment can have very serious results. Prolonged use of any drug generally means a gradual loss of effect with need to increase the dose progressively, when unpleasant side-effects may appear. Any drug which carries a warning against driving while under its influence is certainly useless to a percussionist. He requires reaction times at least as fast as those of the car driver! Some of the most commonly prescribed drugs actually produce tremor if used for any length of time; nothing more need be said of this.

Of the addictive drugs, it seems hardly necessary to say that there must be absolute abstention. Anything which makes the mind hazy is disastrous to a discipline as demanding as orchestral playing. Perhaps the most commonly used drug is alcohol and it is essential to realise that it is not exempt from the changes referred to above. But it has a place, taken in moderation *after* performance. Compared with most drugs, its action is short, and public concern about its abuse is such that everyone must know the safe dossage. As an adjunct to 'unwinding' after the nervous tension of performance it carries little risk and can do much good. Certainly, many fine players have so used it over periods of many years without ill effect. But the older age groups do not tolerate it as well as the younger and dosage may need to be less! It is insufficiently realised that a dose of alcohol insufficient to produce a shaky hand (a tremor) the next morning will still leave the muscles stiff and so prevent proper relaxation.

With other drugs, where the advice of a doctor is obtained (as it always should be), it is essential that a player makes him (or her) fully aware of the demands of his professional work. Only in that way can the most suitable preparation be prescribed, and it is of course sensible to go to a practitioner accustomed to dealing with the problems of musicians, if at all possible.

Apart from alcohol in moderation, drugs are best avoided and regarded very much as a last resort.

A word about posture will not be out of place. Nature designed the back for use in the horizontal position which it occupies in every animal except man. With man, subjecting it to the vertical position, it is so prone to ill-understood physical defects that it is worth taking great care of it. General fitness, as already described, will go a long way but precautions in playing are also essential. Care should be taken not to slouch over a drum kit or adapt the body to an instrument. The instrument must always be adapted to the body, with its infinite variations. As soon as any discomfort is felt in the back, one's playing position should be carefully reviewed. It is often helpful to get someone else to watch you, and to report. You may not like what is said, but it could prove back-preserving!

Finally, for the older player, it must be accepted that some loss of dexterity may occur, perhaps from the mid-fifties onwards. Surgeons and dentists certainly experience this though, as always, there is very great individual variation and some seem to escape almost completely. A 'warm-up' period before playing will be found helpful. Certainly, to maintain best form there is no substitute for the highest attainable level of fitness both mental and physical (consistent with age and any health problems) and regular practice. The man who said 'Oh, I don't practise now, I can play it' really does exist—and certainly can't 'play it'.

# APPENDIX

RECOMMENDED TUTORS and a selection of standard works, with notes, for study and performance, illustrating the technical demands of the normal orchestral repertoire.

*Modern School for Snare Drum:* Morris Goldenberg. (Chappell and Co., New York).

*Modern Techniques for the Progressive Drummer:* Max Abrams. (Premier Drum Company, London; Leicester).

*How to play drums:* James Blades and Johnny Dean. (International Music Publications, London).

*Modern School for Xylophone, Marimba, Vibraphone:* Morris Goldenberg. (Chappell and Co., New York).

*Fundamental Studies for Mallets:* Garwood Whaley. (J.R. Publications, New York).

*Modern Method for Tympani:* Saul Goodman. (Mills Music, New York).

*Musical Studies for the Intermediate Tympanist:* Garwood Whaley. (J.R. Publications, New York).

*Orchestral Percussion Technique:* James Blades. (Oxford University Press, London).

*Percussion Instruments and their History:* James Blades. (Faber and Faber, London).

*Percussion:* James Holland. (In Yehudi Menuhin Music Guides, Macdonald and Jane's, London).

### BACH, HANDEL, HAYDN, MOZART

The orchestral works of these composers form the ideal musical diet upon which the aspiring tympanist should 'cut his teeth' and it is by playing them with an orchestra, rather than by private study and practice that the greatest benefits are obtained, for they are often technically easier than the easiest of exercises in the 'tutors'. In this very simplicity lies their enormous training value. The technique is soon mastered and the novice can devote most of his attention to listening critically to his intonation, tone and the general effect of his contribution to the ensemble—a process which is the secret of good orchestral playing on any instrument.

It is scarcely profitable or possible to single out individual works, but every tympanist should make himself familiar with Mozart's Serenade for Strings and Tympani (K. 239), a charming example of delicate and effective writing for the drums in the classical style. The novice should realize that although the technical demands of these composers' works are modest they are in no sense easy to play well or unrewarding, for almost every note is something of a solo and defects of tone and tuning are very obvious. Conversely, accurate tuning and good tone greatly enhance the beauty of the ensemble.

Haydn in particular had a fine conception of the idiom of the tympani and a good rendering of his parts brings the player a deep satisfaction. As in the performance of all good music, the thoughts of a great mind are being re-created.

*Beethoven: Symphonies No. 1, 3, 5, 7, 8 and 9.*

Here the technical demands are greater, especially in the later symphonies, and a note-perfect performance of the Ninth Symphony is no small accomplishment. The ability to bring out *accents* correctly will develop as well as general beating technique, and private study of the parts is important.

*Brahms: Symphonies No. 1, 2 and 4.*

Here 'gymnastics' are fewer than with Beethoven but the ability to follow an independent line of thought and to play a part sometimes apparently at variance with other sections of the orchestra is developed.

*Dvorak: Symphonies No. 7, 8 and 9.*

These form a useful transition from the classical style of part. In general the technical difficulties are moderate and the parts are rewarding—sometimes thrilling—to play. An occasional change of tuning during the course of a movement is called for.

*Smetana: Overture, 'The Bartered Bride'*

A fine example of a 'standard overture', this work calls for a close, even roll at all dynamic levels on the top F which is used throughout.

*Wagner: Overture 'Tannhauser'*

*Sibelius: 'Finlandia'*

In the parts of these composers the quality of *endurance* becomes important to the tympanist. He must acquire the ability to roll very quietly, and very loudly, and to go on—and on! The secret is to practise rolls at all volumes for periods longer than are ever likely to be required.

### Tschaikowsky: Overture—Fantasy 'Romeo and Juliet'

This is a good representative sample of this composer's very effective scoring for the tympani and percussion. The long solo roll at the end needs special attention.

*Borodin: 'Polovtsian Dances'*

*Rimsky-Korsakov: 'Capriccio Espagnol'*

*Elgar: 'The Dream of Gerontius'*

*Walton: 'Belshazzar's Feast'*

*Stravinsky: 'Rite of Spring'*

*Bartok: 'Concerto for Orchestra' Sonata for two Pianos and Percussion*

These works contain brilliant writing for the tympani and practically every other percussion instrument in normal orchestral use. The technical demands are considerable and their study will give a good general idea of modern trends in scoring for tympani and percussion.